U.S. NAVY
DIVE AND
TORPEDO BOMBERS
OF WWII

BARRETT TILLMAN • ROBERT L. LAWSON

MBI Publishing Company

Dedication

This book is respectfully dedicated to Harry Gann, a mentor, great naval aviation historian, and above all, a wonderful friend.

First published in 2001 by MBI Publishing Company,
Galtier Plaza, Suite 200, 380 Jackson Street
St. Paul, MN 55101-3885 USA

MBI Publishing Company books are also available at discounts in bulk quantity for industrial or sales-promotional use. For details write to Special Sales Manager at Motorbooks International Wholesalers & Distributors, Galtier Plaza, Suite 200, 380 Jackson Street, St. Paul, MN 55101-3885 USA

Front Cover: The big Curtiss SB2C was known by various nicknames—"Duece," "SB Duecy" and "Beast"—along with some unprintable ones. Although it replaced the SBD in the fleet it never received the acceptance and acclaim by its aircrews that it's predecessor had. Ordnance men load 20mm ammunition into a factory-fresh SB2C-4 (BuNo 65254) c. 1944. USN photo, courtesy Hal Andrews

Frontispiec:e Marine 2nd LT Carlton Compher prepares to dismount his VMBT-233 TBM-3 following a 5 June 1945 close-air-support mission during the Okinawa campaign 5 June 1945. VMBT-233 was a unit of MCVG-1 at the time, assigned to Block Island (CVE-106). USMC photo

Title page: The Dauntless entered World War II when VB-6 and VS-6 SBD-2s and -3s launched from Enterprise (CV-6) on 7 Dec 1941. CV-6's air group inadvertently flew into the middle of the Japanese raid on Pearl Harbor that initiated the U.S. into the war. Enterprise Air Group SBDs and Douglas TBD-1s are spotted for launch during 1941. USN photo

Back Cover, top: "The indispensable man" was the carrier's landing signal officer. A naval aviator himself, the LSO guided his fellow airmen during the final stages of landing by a standard set of signals he gave with his paddles. Many a wounded, frightened, and/or fatigued pilot owed his life to the LSO who brought him safely aboard. Lt(jg) Walter F. Wujcik works pilot aboard Bellau Wood (CVL-24) in 1945. USN photo

Back cover, bottom: As new models of the Dauntless began reporting to the fleet, the SBD-1s went to the training command. Naval Aviation Operational Training Command -1 in flight c. 1943. USN photo

Library of Congress Cataloging-in-Publication Data

Tillman, Barrett.
    U.S. Navy dive and torpedo bombers of World War II/Barrett Tillman & Robert L. Lawson.
        p. cm.
    Includes bibliographical references and index.
    ISBN 0-7603-0959-0 (hc.: alk. paper)
    1. Dive bombers--History--20th century. 2. Torpedo bombers--United States--History--20th century. 3 World War, 1939-1945--Aerial operations, American. 4. World War, 1939-1945--Naval operations, American. I. Lawson, Robert L.

UG1242.A28 T55 2001
623.7'463--dc21

Edited by Mike Haenggi
Designed by Katie Sonmor

Printed in China

Contents

Chapter one

Scout-Bombers and Torpedo Planes

When Junkers 87 Stukas of the Luftwaffe led the blitzkrieg into Poland in September 1939, the American military could only watch in wonder. The awesome professionalism of Germany's armed forces had welded air and ground components into an integrated, seemingly unstoppable instrument of focused violence.

Ironically, much of the Nazi air force's ground-support doctrine had been absorbed from the U.S. Marine Corps, the result of Germany's close observation of American military aviation during the 1930s. Though the flying leathernecks still had a long way to go before achieving full integration along German lines, the concept and execution of close air support had been laid. American naval aviators had especially impressed their foreign counterparts with their precision dive-bombing, and the lessons were quickly absorbed.

However, the U.S. Navy lagged far behind its potential enemies in quality of hardware. When the Second World War erupted that fall, 50 percent of the scout-bombers, torpedo planes, and fighters in carrier squadrons were still biplanes. Nor was there much com-

As America entered World War II, most SBCs had been transferred to the Naval Air Reserve. NARU Brooklyn SBC-4s were photographed by Rudy Arnold during a 1940 flight. *Courtesy Stan Piet*

Fleet deliveries of the TBD-1 began in October 1937 to VT-3, and by mid-1938 the plane would equip five carrier squadrons. VT-5's 5-T-7 is pictured here over a then-barren San Diego County countryside during a training flight c. 1938. VT-5, along with VT-2, fought the first carrier-vs.-carrier battle during May 1942 at the Battle of Coral Sea. *USN photo*

monality. All four carrier-based torpedo squadrons flew the Douglas TBD-1 Devastator, but navy scout-bomber units operated four types of aircraft: three squadrons with Vought SB2U Vindicator monoplanes; three with Curtiss SBC Helldiver biplanes; two with Vought SBU biplanes and another partly formed with SBCs and SBUs; plus two squadrons with the most modern type, Northrop's BT dive-bomber.

These disparate elements amounted to 91 scouts, 75 dive-bombers, and 69 torpedo planes—235 aircraft, including 89 biplanes, aboard five carriers: *Lexington* (CV-2), *Saratoga* (CV-3), *Ranger* (CV-4), *Yorktown* (CV-5), and *Enterprise* (CV-6). Another flattop, the new *Wasp* (CV-7), was not yet commissioned. Meanwhile, one fighting squadron was slowly re-equipping with monoplane Brewster F2A Buffalos; the others retained Grumman F2Fs or F3Fs.

At the same time, Marine Corps tactical aviation was 100 percent biplanes, and technologically nearly a decade behind the navy. With just six combat squadrons in two air groups at Quantico, Virginia, and San Diego, California, the leathernecks owned about 30 Great Lakes BG-1 dive-bombers and a dozen wheeled Curtiss SOC-3 Seamew scouts. The corps' two fighting squadrons flew Grumman F3F-2s while the "cats and dogs" in utility and administrative units added another 64 aircraft to the total.

Fifteen months later the navy and the nation went to general quarters on 7 December, 1941. A half-century after that Sunday morning, historians were still debating whether the Roosevelt administration was guilty of treasonable malfeasance or criminal neglect, but 386 aircraft from six Japanese carriers astonished America and the world with a spectacular surprise attack on Pearl Harbor, Territory of Hawaii. By then, U.S. naval aviation was better prepared to go to war, but still had to play catch-up from an initial deficit.

Two more carriers, *Wasp* and *Hornet* (CV-8), were commissioned and operational since summer 1939. The numbers of scout-bombers and torpedo planes in navy air groups had grown from 235 to 334, and quality was improved among the bombing units, which now had 158 Douglas SBD-2 and -3 Dauntlesses. But SB2U Vindicators remained in scouting squadrons assigned to the Atlantic Fleet.

The same TBD-1 torpedo plane remained from before, but in greater numbers: 60 equipping four full "TorpRons" in *Lexington*, *Saratoga*, *Yorktown*, and *Enterprise*, plus cadres in *Ranger*, *Wasp*, and *Hornet*. The latter, expected to inaugurate the Grumman TBF Avenger to fleet service, still struggled with an assortment of Devastators and Naval Aircraft Factory SBNs.

Deployable Marine Corps scout-bombers had more than doubled in number from a year and a half previously, with 100 SB2Us and SBDs on hand, plus a dozen biplane SBCs. Force expansion had reached 12 squadrons within the two air groups, of which nine squadrons were presumably capable of combat service.

The tactical organization of navy and marine squadrons was similar: nominally 18 aircraft organized into three-plane sections and six-plane divisions. The skipper was ordinarily a lieutenant commander, though full commanders and "bull lieutenants" led combat squadrons during the first year of hostilities. Marine squadrons were commanded by captains or majors, equivalent to their navy counterparts. Inevitably the COs

Rare 1941 color photos of Pacific Fleet carrier aircraft depict VB-3 Vought SB2U-1s and a VB-6 BT-1 during the filming of the epic motion picture *Dive Bomber*. The upper photo was taken on board *Enterprise* (CV-6), where much of the at-sea action was filmed. CV-6 is at NAS San Diego (now NAS North Island) with Lindbergh Field in the background. Above is the east field flight line at NAS San Diego. SB2U Vindicators (better known as "wind indicators") were in three carrier squadrons at war's outbreak. *Jerry Litwak coll., courtesy AAHS and Harry Gann*

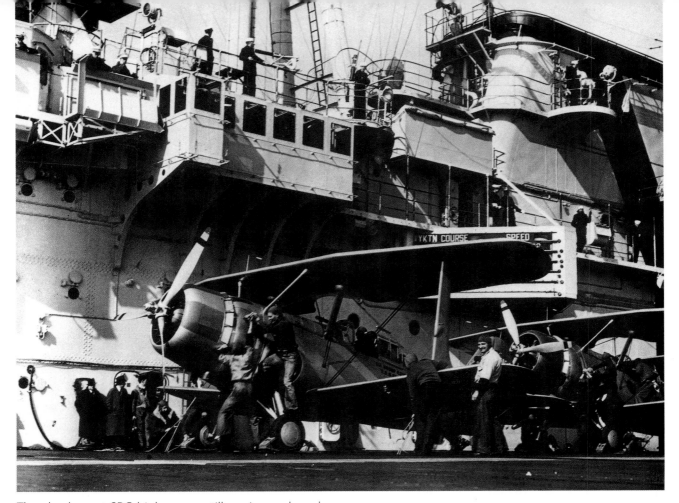

The obsolescent SBC biplane was still serving on board U.S. carriers at the time of the Japanese attack on Pearl Harbor, although most of the 186 navy Helldivers were in the training command. The *Enterprise* Air Group commander, Lt. Comdr. Giles E. Short, prepares to start his SBC-3's engine on board CV-6 during an October 1938 fleet exercise with *Yorktown* (CV-5). *USN photo*

were career professionals, products of the "trade school," the U.S. Naval Academy at Annapolis, Maryland.

Prewar carrier doctrine for attacks on a major enemy surface force emphasized coordination between dive-bombers and torpedo planes. Because of the relatively slow approach speed of the TBD—a net rate of advance of less than 100 knots against a 30-knot target—the Dauntlesses were expected to attack first. Accurate dive-bombing could not only inflict significant damage itself, but could provide much-needed cover and diversion for the torpedo squadron's approach. Where enemy fighter interception was expected, Grumman F4F Wildcats nearly always provided closer escort to the torpedo planes because the Dauntlesses were better able to defend themselves, and their high-altitude approach rendered them less vulnerable.

A doctrinal, set-piece attack, however, worked only once in the first year of the war. During the Battle of the Coral Sea in May 1942, the *Lexington* and *Yorktown* air groups coordinated exceptionally well, putting nearly 100 aircraft over the enemy force and sinking the light carrier *Shoho* on the 7th. The next day, however, poor weather in the target area prevented such coordination, and some units never located the two larger Japanese flattops.

No comparable bombing-torpedo attacks were mounted in the next three carrier duels at Midway, the Eastern Solomons, or Santa Cruz. Part of the reason was attributable to the Japanese habit of wide dispersal of available forces, which tended to dissipate the strike aircraft available to the always-outnumbered Americans. An additional factor was the irony of increased fighter strength aboard U.S. carriers but proportionately fewer strike escorts. The original 18-plane fighting squadrons were insufficient to meet both escort and fleet defense requirements, and where a hard choice had to be made, task group commanders nearly always favored their ForceCAPs to protect priceless flight decks. Consequently, most 1942 carrier operations proceeded with little or no fighter escort.

The subject already had been addressed in the Navy Bureau of Aeronautics. Only a week after Pearl Harbor the VSB design bureau predicted that attack aircraft would need fighter escort and therefore a single-seat dive-bomber was warranted. A weight and performance benefit would ensue if the gunner's position were eliminated.

Similarly, the VTB bureau advocated development of a large, strong, multipurpose aircraft that would incorporate all the carrier attack missions. While the VTSB designation was proposed but never adopted, the path had been cleared for a generic single-seat attack aircraft. Letters were sent to Curtiss and Douglas, soliciting design proposals that eventually led to the superb AD-1 Skyraider. But that was a postwar development. In the meantime, the navy would fight a global conflict with aircraft on hand or already under development.

NEW SHIPS, NEW PLANES

By mid-1943 the situation had improved considerably. Though Dauntlesses remained the scout-bombers, Avengers had fully replaced TBDs, while F6F Hellcats afforded both a numerical and qualitative improvement in the "VF" component. Earlier that year, air group composition had been streamlined from four squadrons to three by incorporating the scouts into the bombing squadron. From an operating viewpoint it made no difference, as the VB/VS missions were fully interchangeable.

Operating side by side with the 27,000-ton *Essex* (CV-9)-class carriers were *Independence*-class (CVL-23) light carriers built on cruiser hulls. These nine ships, as fast as the *Essexes*, embarked fewer aircraft arranged in two-squadron air groups. Hellcats and Avengers were the only types deployed in CVLs, which had insufficient deck or hangar space for dive-bombers. The Dauntless had nonfolding wings, and the Curtiss SB2C Helldiver, which entered combat in November 1943, was simply too large.

A similar arrangement existed in escort carriers (CVEs), which typically embarked a unified composite squadron of fighters and torpedo planes. Here again, Avengers provided all the heavy attack capability while Wildcats or Hellcats filled the fighter role. As a generality, in the Pacific the CVEs were optimized for close air

Bombing Squadron 8 operated SBC-4s during the war maneuvers held during August 1941 in South Carolina. Here, BuNo 4284 is carrying special markings used for the games while in formation with Fighting 8 Grumman F4F-3A Wildcats. *USN photo*

Although World War II had started in Europe in September 1939 with Germany's attack on Poland, the United States had virtually sat on the sidelines until Japanese carrier forces attacked Pearl Harbor 7 December 1941. As a result of this attack, the U.S. Navy suffered its worst defeat in history, and the course of naval warfare was changed forever. At left, *Arizona's* (BB-39) ammunition magazines explode after receiving hits from dive-bombers. Above, dramatic results of the Japanese attack are seen in the view of battleship row at Ford Island. *USN photos, courtesy Don Montgomery*

support of amphibious operations, while Atlantic "jeep carriers" specialized in antisubmarine warfare. In either case, Grumman had a near-monopoly on both missions, as CVEs flew F4F/FM Wildcats and F6Fs along with TBF/TBMs until 1945 when Marine Corps squadrons deployed with Vought F4U Corsairs.

From late 1942 until late 1943, the typical fleet carrier embarked 36 fighters, 36 bombers, and 18 torpedo planes. But the increasing need for additional fighters permitted no amendment to the immutable law of carrier operations—space is always at a premium. Therefore, by the time of the Saipan operation in June 1944 a big-deck air group typically owned 40 fighters. That August, prior to the Philippines campaign, 54 Hellcats forced further reductions to 24 Helldivers (which had fully replaced Dauntlesses in July) and 18 Avengers.

Several Vought SB2U Vindicators were used by CAGs as their personal aircraft, such as Lt. Comdr. Oscar A. Weller's SB2U-1. BuNo 0773 is wearing the bright green tail and CAG stripe color of *Ranger* (CV-4) in this 29 May 1940 photo. This aircraft was lost in a crash 29 July 1941 while assigned to VS-42. *James C. Fahey, courtesy Wm. T. Larkins*

When World War II began in 1939, U.S. Marine Corps tactical aviation was 100 percent biplanes. With only six combat squadrons in two air groups at MCAS Quantico, Virginia, and NAS San Diego, California, the leather-necks' attack capability consisted of only about 30 Great Lakes BG-1 dive-bombers. VB-6M BG-1 BuNo 9840 is over San Diego area 14 October 1935. *USN photo*

Soon after the U.S. Navy entered World War II, VT-8 was operating as a split unit—one component was at Norfolk preparing to receive the new TBF-1 to replace its TBD-1s operating from *Hornet* (CV-8). As an interim measure, the Norfolk detachment flew Naval Aircraft Factory SBN-1 production versions of the Brewster SBA-1 design. VT-8 SBN-1 is pictured here over Norfolk 12 February 1942. *USN photo, courtesy Hal Andrews*

Nor was that the end of it. By year-end the *kamikaze* crisis raised an *Essex*-class air group to 73 fighters, with 15 each of SB2Cs and TBMs. After Leyte Gulf, in some ships, the VB squadron was put ashore to provide more operating room for Hellcats and Corsairs, which could perform adequate dive-bombing. The operational training syllabus for fighters was expanded to include more emphasis on air-ground

The first U.S. Navy attack plane to enter combat in World War II was Lt. Comdr. Howard L. "Brigham" Young's SBD-2 BuNo 2162. The *Enterprise* (CV-6) CAG was leading his air group's SBDs into Ford Island 7 December 1941 when they flew into the middle of the Japanese attack on Pearl Harbor. *USN photo, courtesy Harry Gann*

ordnance, while only Avengers could continue to provide the aerial torpedo option.

Throughout the Pacific War, one of the main differences between Japanese and American operating procedures was reconnaissance. The Imperial Navy preferred to retain most of its carrier bombers for offensive missions, relying more upon battleship or cruiser-based floatplanes as scouts. In 1942, the U.S. Navy, with one-quarter of its carrier squadrons composed of scouting units, took the opposite tack. A typical search team was composed of two Dauntlesses flying a wedge-shaped search sector to a distance of 200 or occasionally 250 miles.

By 1944, however, Hellcats, Avengers, and late-model Helldivers possessed sufficient range for previously impossible carrier-based searches. A tactical radius of 400 miles was not unknown, often flown by mixed sections of a TBM or SB2C with an F6F escort. In some cases, radio relay flights were required midway between the task force and the far end of the search sector in order to provide timely information. Though bombers and torpedo planes flew these lengthy searches with light ordnance loads—or none at all—their range, coupled with onboard radar, gave air operations planners an option seldom imagined only two years before.

Saratoga (CV-3) introduced the Douglas TBD-1 into combat when two VT-2 aircraft attacked a Japanese submarine 10 December 1941 off Johnston Island, southwest of Oahu. *Sara* steams with Air Group 12's SBD-5s and TBF-1/1C and TBM-1Cs embarked during January 1944. *USN photo*

Enterprise (CV-6), along with Saratoga (CV-3) and Ranger (CV-4), were the only prewar fast carriers to survive the war. Enterprise fought in every major campaign in the Pacific except the battle of Coral Sea and earned more battle stars than any other carrier. CV-6 steams en route to the Panama Canal from Pearl Harbor with CVG-55(N) embarked during October 1945. *USN photo*

The naval armament treaty of 1922 caused Wasp's (CV-7) design size to be held to only 14,700 tons. Weight-saving compromises in her design contributed to her loss after being torpedoed off Guadalcanal 15 September 1942. Seen here in Casco Bay, Maine, in early 1942, she has VS-71 and -72 SB2Us embarked as her attack component. *USN photo*

THE OPPOSITION

By comparison, Japanese carrier aircraft from the outset possessed greater range than the Americans. The Dauntless' and Devastator's opposite numbers, the Aichi D3A "Val" and Nakajima B5N "Kate," (so named in mid-1943) reflected the Imperial Navy's emphasis on strike radius. Additionally, a doctrinal difference in search procedure gave much of the responsibility to float-planes based aboard battleships and cruisers, thus freeing bombers and torpedo planes for attack missions.

Both the Val and Kate were supplanted by newer types in 1943–1944, but neither was completely replaced,

as were the Devastator in 1942 and the Dauntless in 1944. The Kate's successor was the same firm's B6N *Tenzan* (Heavenly Mountain), capable of more than 250 knots (over 290 miles per hour), and possessed of almost twice the B5N's range. The *Tenzan* became known to Allied fliers as Jill, and its size and high landing speed limited its use to large carriers from late 1943. Production totaled nearly 1,300 in two models.

Following the fixed-gear Val was Yokosuka's modern D4Y *Suisei* (Comet) dive-bomber. Designed with a 12-cylinder liquid-cooled engine, the *Suisei* also was a 300-knot aircraft in the "dash three" and "dash four" models

Hornet (CV-8) was the last of the prewar carriers to be commissioned before Pearl Harbor. Unfortunately, she would serve the least amount of time. Commissioned 20 October 1941, she was sunk 26 October 1942 during the Battle of Santa Cruz. *USN photo*

LEFT MIDDLE:
The ships that defined carrier aviation were the magnificent 24 *Essex*-class ships built between 1941 and 1950. Their flight decks varied from the short-hull 860-foot design to the long-hull 878-foot one. They were designed to carry as many as 100 aircraft. Here, *Essex* (CV-9) steams during mid-1943 with CVG-9 embarked. VB-9's SBD-4/5s are spotted aft with VF-9's F6F-3s and VT-9's TBF-1/1Cs forward. *USN photo*

using air-cooled radials. The different power plants may have caused some recognition problems, but U.S. Navy pilots identified both types as "Judy." The most numerous Japanese naval attack aircraft, 2,030 *Suisei* were produced by Aichi and one of the naval arsenals between 1942 and 1945.

Aside from performance figures, perhaps the greatest statistic among all these Japanese carrier bombers or torpedo planes is that their total number was lower than the number of Dauntlesses. Combined with Avengers and Helldivers, the discrepancy amounted to a factor of almost four times in favor of the U.S. Navy.

Whatever their numbers, throughout the Pacific War, Japanese carrier- and land-based aircraft sank 37 U.S. Navy warships (excluding U.S. submarines), compared to

Born from a need for small transports, the CVE escort carriers proved as valuable as their larger contemporaries in a variety of missions. *Santee* (CVE-29), with VGF-29 F4F-4 Wildcats, along with VGS-29 TBF-1 Avengers and SBD Dauntlesses is seen in mid-1943. *USN photo*

Curtiss' follow-on Helldiver was the XSB2C-1 that was first flown 18 December 1940. The prototype crashed when its engine failed on landing and was rebuilt only to be destroyed during a 21 December test dive when the right wing and tail failed. *Rudy Arnold/NASM, courtesy Stan Piet*

Independence (CVL-22) was the first of nine World War II fast carriers that were built from cruiser hulls. VC-22's SBDs, seen here 15 July 1943, were replaced with TBF-1s by September. *USN photo, courtesy A. D. Baker*

This early war photo shows the makeup of *Wasp's* (CV-7) Air Group during the battle for Guadalcanal. VS-71/72 SBD-3s are spotted aft with VF-71 F4F-4s prior to launch just a few days before the prewar carrier's sinking on 15 September 1942. VT-71's TBF-1s are absent. *Lt. (jg) John R. Pramm, courtesy T.J. Wilkes*

the 23 sunk by Japanese submarines and the 24 by surface ships. Nearly twice as many American ships were destroyed by bombs as aerial torpedoes, while suicide aircraft were nearly as destructive as bombs and torpedoes combined. Clearly, the enemy possessed a strong, capable air weapon against which the Pacific Fleet had to match itself.

CLOSE AIR SUPPORT, USMC STYLE

Meanwhile the Marine Corps had perfected its own joint operations doctrine. A seemingly complex command and control structure was established by 1943, with ground and airborne controllers capable of directing "flying leathernecks" to precision weapons delivery against targets that were often invisible from the air. The

As the navy began its offensive operations in the Pacific, it placed emphasis on attack aircraft, as evidenced by the number of SBD-3s of VB/VS-9, assigned to CVG-9 embarked in *Essex* (CV-9) during fall 1943. *USN photo*

Japanese mastery of camouflage frequently rendered such techniques necessary, and specialized training was required for ground observers to describe terrain features recognizable to a pilot. With training and practice, however, marine aviators were capable of putting bombs and napalm within rifle or even pistol shot of American front-line troops.

For a specific operation, such as the seizure of an enemy-occupied island, the marines designated an overall commander of support aircraft. Typically, he was a senior aviator (not always a marine) responsible for allocating fighter and bomber squadrons to support the assault troops. An air control center received requests from infantry units and dispatched formations to the appropriate area, where they established radio contact with the air liaison party (ALP). The on-scene ALP, in turn, provided

tactical information to the formation leader, ensuring that friendly forces were well identified by recognition panels, colored smoke, or other methods.

A representative mission occurred on Bougainville in November 1943, when 17 Dauntlesses and 12 Avengers attacked Piva Village, a fortified position holding up the marine advance. The bombers obliterated the village, permitting the infantry to occupy the area with minimum casualties. Essentially, that was the philosophy behind close air support: minimizing friendly losses.

Perhaps the ultimate example of close air support occurred on Peleliu in 1944. Operating from a rough airstrip on the contested island, marine pilots sometimes had no time to raise their landing gear before bombing or strafing Japanese positions on rocky crags lined with caves. Increasingly, air-delivered napalm was used to cover an area known

During mid- to late 1943, VC-25 (VT-25 after 15 December 1943) operated a mix of SBD-4s and -5s along with TBF-1/1Cs while embarked in *Cowpens* (CVL-25). *USN photo*

Close air support (CAS) for the ground troops was the name of the game for World War II marine Dauntless pilots. Perhaps the ultimate example of CAS was during the Peleliu campaign in 1944. Operating from a dirt airstrip, Marine pilots on occasion had no time to raise their landing gear before bombing or strafing Japanese positions. Pictured here are VMSB-234 "Flying Goldbricks" SBD-4s of the marine's 16th Defense Battalion on an April 1943 mission out of Palmyra Island. *USMC photo by Sgt. T. Schlossenberg*

to contain hidden enemy positions that were relatively impervious to precision attacks with bombs or rockets.

In the Philippines campaign of 1944–1945, Marine Corps Dauntlesses supported the army's drive on Manila by guarding the First Cavalry Division's right flank—from the air. Relatively few strike sorties were necessary owing to the rapidity of the Cav's advance, but constant aerial surveillance by the Dauntless air crews provided

Grumman Iron Works aircraft dominated the CVL air groups after the phaseout of Douglas SBDs from the CVLGs in late 1943 and early 1944. *Monterey's* (CVL-26) VT-30, seen here preparing for a Gilberts raid in late 1943, operated only TBFs and TBMs with CVLG-30. *USN photo*

priceless intelligence on Japanese positions. Thus alerted, the cavalrymen could bypass strong points, which were mopped up later.

Eventually, the methods employed by Dauntless, Avenger, and Helldiver squadrons in World War II become codified in Marine Corps doctrine for later conflicts: "Never send a man where you can send a bomb."

The vast experience obtained from 1942 to 1945 solidified the methods and doctrine of close air support in conflicts to come. Indeed, during the desperate retreat down the Korean Peninsula in 1950, the Navy and Marine Corps profited enormously from the integrated components of a close-knit air-ground team. At a time when the U.S. Army and Air Force often were unable to talk to each other, naval aviators and marine riflemen could communicate on common radio frequencies in a language that both clearly understood: the language of tactical air power. That ability was in large part responsible for the successful withdrawal from the Chosin Reservoir against appalling odds in the face of hundreds of thousands of Communist Chinese troops.

However, the air-ground efficiency established between the navy and marines did not always function so well. As the Cold War heightened during the late 1950s and flared to the flash point in Southeast Asia in the early 1960s, the U.S. Navy found itself playing catch-up. By far the greatest threat was the Soviet Union with its own massive nuclear arsenal. Consequently, the emphasis on nuclear weapons delivery by navy attack squadrons resulted in less training for conventional warfare—exactly the type of mission required in Vietnam. Navy squadron and air wing training had to be revised to change the emphasis from the strategic to the tactical, though the Marine Corps retained most of its previous tactical air power ability with emphasis on close air support. It was no surprise, as the lieutenants, lieutenant commanders, and majors of the 1940s became the navy captains and admirals and marine colonels and generals of the 1960s and 1970s.

In the end, naval aviation's focus came full circle. From Douglas Dauntlesses to McDonnell Douglas Skyhawks, from Grumman Avengers to Grumman Intruders, the mission of carrier-based attack aviation remained the same: Project power ashore by precision delivery of conventional ordnance. Nearly 60 years later, the heritage established by the World War II generation of naval attack aviation remains undiminished.

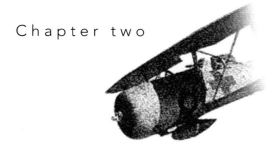

Chapter two

Douglas SBD Dauntless

Ironically, the most successful naval strike aircraft of the Second World War owed its origin to a U.S. Army airplane. Northrop Aircraft produced a series of progressive designs during the 1930s, both for naval and military use. The evolutionary development leading from a land-based army attack aircraft to a carrier-based dive-bomber spanned more than a period of years—it defined an era.

Edward H. Heinemann had an exceptional background as a young aeronautical engineer. Largely self-taught, he worked for Douglas, International, Moreland, Northrop, and Lockheed between 1926 and 1931 before settling with Jack Northrop's new El Segundo operation in early 1932. He was not yet 24 years old. As a draftsman he contributed to the Gamma and Delta monoplanes—record-setting aircraft for altitude and distance. Heinemann's first navy project at El Segundo was the prototype XFT-1 carrier fighter, which was never purchased.

NORTHROP'S DIVE-BOMBER

The firm's XBT-1 dive-bomber, however, was another matter. Based upon the layout of the army A-17 attack aircraft of 1934, with a similar airfoil, it competed with five other companies for the navy contract, including Curtiss, Vought, and Grumman. Heinemann's main contribution to the BT was the dive brakes, which carried over to the Douglas SBD Dauntless.

In evaluating the naval dive-bomber, test pilot Vance Breese reported serious tail flutter during steep dives, requiring a search for more information. To accomplish this aim, Heinemann rode in the radioman-gunner's seat of the prototype, facing aft while filming the tail surfaces. He said in his memoir, "I don't think there is anyone who has made more 9-G pullouts than Vance Breese and myself." The vortex generated by the flaps caused frightening excursions of the horizontal stabilizer, threatening structural failure of the empennage.

The most numerous version of the Dauntless was the SBD-5—2,965 went to the Navy and another 675 to the AAF. They had a Wright R-1820-60 engine that brought the horsepower up to 1,200 from previous models' 1,000. An internally mounted reflector bombsight solved the problem of fogging, commonly suffered by external sights in moist tropical conditions. The -5s began rolling off Douglas production lines in February 1943. *Douglas photo, courtesy Harry Gann*

The aircraft that would arguably become the finest dive-bomber of World War II, as well as the Navy's pride and joy, ironically began life as an Army Air Corps design of 1934, the Northrop A-17 Shrike. A long evolution period ensued during which Northrop produced the BT-1, which entered the fleet in 1938. An amalgamation of Northrop and Douglas facilities next produced the SBD Dauntless of 1940. Only three squadrons operated the BT-1, VB-5 (above), VB-3, and VB-6, all for only short periods. *USN photo*

In an unusual move, the Navy gave all 57 SBD-1s to the Marine Corps, the first of which went to VMB-2 in June 1940. VMB-2 commanding officer's SBD-1, BuNo 1597, is in flight 2 August 1940 over southern California. VMB-2 became VMSB-232 on 1 July 1941. Red, white, and blue rudder stripes were USMC markings and were deleted in 1941. *Douglas photo, courtesy Harry Gann*

VMB-2 SBD-1, BuNo 1741, awaits delivery on Douglas' El Segundo, California, flight line, c. November 1940. The dash one had two fixed .30-caliber guns in the nose and one .30-caliber free gun in the aft cockpit. *Douglas photo, courtesy Harry Gann*

Stymied for a solution, Northrop consulted the National Advisory Committee for Aeronautics (NACA). An NACA representative, Charles Helm, suggested the alternating-vortex theory, which potentially could reduce a large vortex off the solid flaps by punching holes in them.

It worked. After progressively drilling more 3-inch holes in the flaps, the XBT-1 became a relatively well-behaved dive-bomber with a terminal velocity of 250 knots.

Other flaws had to be cured while the XBT-1 was evaluated at NAS Anacostia, Maryland. The Pratt &

Whitney R-1534 of 700 horsepower gulped raw fuel through the carburetor during prolonged dives, leading to spectacular "torching." The problem was cured, as were the cracking of the Plexiglas canopy and landing gear locks in cold climates.

A weather-beaten VMB-132 SBD-1 shows the effects of the increased wartime preparation operations of 1941. This model of the Dauntless had a Wright R-1820-32 engine and a top speed of 253 miles per hour. It carried 180 gallons of fuel internally and a 1,200-pound bomb load. *USMC photo*

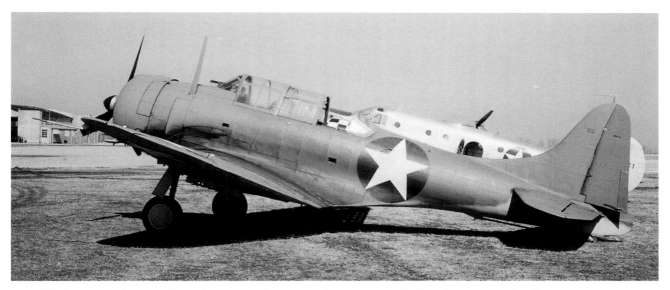

The SBD-2, produced for the Navy, had longer legs with a fuel capacity of 260 gallons internally, plus the capability for an external tank. Bombing 2, assigned to *Lexington* (CV-2), received the first of this model in November 1940. This SBD-2 is at Monroe, Louisiana, in late 1942. *Fred Bamburger*

In 1936 Northrop and Vought received contracts for 54 production BT-1s and SB2U-1s, respectively. The Vought, later named Vindicator, entered service in late 1937, with a production run of some 260 airframes including foreign sales. Meanwhile, the first BT-1s were delivered to the fleet in spring 1938. No additional Northrops were ordered, but by September 1939 the *Yorktown* and *Enterprise* bombing squadrons each operated 18 BT-1s with engines uprated to 825 horsepower.

In the interim, corporate changes pointed the way to the Dauntless. When Northrop's El Segundo division was sold to Douglas Aircraft, the latter took over

The SBD-2 had a Wright R-1820-32 engine producing a maximum air speed of 252 miles per hour. The 87 that were produced had outboard wing racks added. *Douglas photo, courtesy Harry Gann*

development of the follow-on dive-bomber, the BT-2. Following a series of changes requested by the Navy Bureau of Aeronautics—most notably engine, landing gear, empennage, and canopy—the company signed a production contract in April 1939. The BT-1's Pratt & Whitney was replaced by Wright's R-1820, a 950-horsepower radial in the SBD-1. First flight was 1 May 1940, the same month as that of Vought's sensational XF4U-1 Corsair fighter.

ENTER THE DAUNTLESS

The initial Dauntless contract was unusual in that it provided for 57 "dash ones" and 87 "dash twos." The original batch was intended for the U.S. Marine Corps, which had been accustomed to hand-me-down navy aircraft approximately forever. The two marine scout-bombing squadrons that first received SBD-1s in summer 1940 were then flying Great Lakes BG-1s, 160-knot biplanes dating from 1933. Never before had the leathernecks been the original recipient of a new aircraft.

Resplendent in their factory-new paint jobs, a formation of SBD-2s is over southern California on a Douglas publicity photo mission, c. early 1941. *Douglas photo, courtesy Harry Gann*

However, there was a reason behind the navy's seeming largesse. Internal fuel for the SBD-1 was only 180 gallons: sufficient for barely three hours' endurance under operational conditions. The theory held that Marine Corps aircraft would be based close behind the infantry battalions they were assigned to support, hence requiring little need for additional range. The SBD-2 navy version held 260 gallons internally, plus having the capability for an external fuel tank. *Lexington's* Bombing Two received its dash twos in November 1940.

Meanwhile, 174 SBD-3s had been ordered in September, with many more to follow. Named "Dauntless" before year-end, the SBD might have ended its production life with completion of the third batch had not six Japanese aircraft carriers attacked the Territory of Hawaii on 7 December 1941. For the next 12 months, neither the navy nor the marines could obtain too many scout-bombers—nor could the U.S. Army Air Forces.

When "dash three" deliveries began in March 1941, the USAAF realized its lack of comparable aircraft. Consequently, later that year the army obtained 78 Dauntlesses directly from the El Segundo production line. They were called SBD-3As by the navy, and the army designated them A-24 Banshees. They were followed by 170 A-24A (SBD-4) and 616 B models (SBD-5) built at Douglas' Tulsa, Oklahoma, plant for a total of 863 Banshees.

Army Air Forces combat use of the Douglas dive-bomber was extremely limited. A group of 52 intended for defense of the Philippines was diverted to Australia, and many of them were lost in the futile defense of the Dutch East Indies during early 1942. However, the "backwater war" of the Central Pacific occupied some A-24s from late 1943 well into 1944, especially in the Marshall Islands.

The USAAF declared the Douglas dive-bomber of marginal utility, however, and disbanded its A-24 squadrons or re-equipped them with other aircraft. The irony was not lost on marine aircrews who found themselves flying direct support missions for the army in a variety of Pacific campaigns—most notably the seizure of Luzon in the Philippines. The "obsolete" Dauntlesses were valued not only for their precision bombing but for the institutional knowledge and doctrine that enabled them to operate so effectively with ground forces.

Aircraft camouflage schemes and markings went through a series of changes during 1940–1942. On 20 August 1941, Commander Aircraft Battle Force directed that all carrier-based aircraft under his command would be painted nonspecular light gray underneath and nonspecular blue-gray on upper surfaces. Red/white rudder stripes were added with a larger national insignia on 5 January 1942. *Douglas photo, courtesy Harry Gann*

Douglas began delivery of the first of 584 navy -3 Dauntlesses in March 1941. Another batch of 78 was delivered to the AAF under the navy designation of SBD-3A, and army designation of A-24 Banshee. VS-5 SBD-3 assigned to *Yorktown* Air Group over the East Coast in late 1944. *USN photo, courtesy NASM*

The SBD was a project that totally absorbed those involved in designing and building it; Ed Heinemann's wife, Lillian, typed the first draft of the pilot's operating handbook. Heinemann himself singled out service engineer Lew Whittier as a devoted Douglas aircraftsman when it was learned that a carrier was deploying from San Diego without spare Dauntless tailhooks. Whittier crammed as many hooks as possible in his own car and drove south with his foot on the floor, barely reaching North Island before the flattop left the pier.

WARTIME VERSIONS

In December 1941, 38 BT-1s remained on the navy inventory, most at NAS Miami, Florida, for operational training. Meanwhile, the navy deployed 199 SBD-2s and -3s in four fleet carriers plus various other units while two marine squadrons flew SBD-1s and -2s in VMSB-132 and -232.

At the time of Pearl Harbor, few U.S. Navy aircraft were fully combat ready. Most had been delivered without self-sealing fuel tanks that limited battle damage, and many still lacked armor plate. Fleet squadrons scrambled to install such features in the lull after 7 December.

In the Pacific Fleet, carrier squadrons were in a constant state of readiness and training. Pilots frequently

At the time of Pearl Harbor, few U.S. Navy aircraft were fully combat ready. Most of them had been delivered without self-sealing fuel tanks, and many lacked armor plate. A VS-41 SBD-3 prepares for launch from *Ranger* (CV-4) during June 1942 workups. *USN photo*

logged 40 or more flight hours per month, including bombing both day and night, gunnery, formation tactics, instrument flying, and carrier procedures. The pace only increased after the Pearl Harbor attack: the logbook of Lt. Richard H. Best of *Enterprise's* Bombing Six shows nearly 100 hours in December, averaging nearly 50 per

A *Ranger* (CV-4) LSO watches a VS-41 SBD-3 after giving the pilot the "cut" signal for landing on board. *USN photo*

Another VS-41 SBD-3 safely touches down on *Ranger's* (CV-4) flight deck as the LSO watches and grades the pilot's landing performance. After each recovery, pilot landing techniques are critiqued by the LSO in the various squadron ready rooms. *USN photo*

On the East Coast, the Dauntless entered combat during Operation Torch, the Allied invasion of North Africa in November 1942 with *Ranger's* (CV-4) Air Group 41 and several CVE-class carriers. VGF and VGS-26 SBD-3s and Grumman F4F-4 Wildcats are on board *Sangamon* (ACV-26) (CVE-26 after 15 July 1943) just prior to the invasion. The aircraft have yellow surround markings on the national insignia that were used specifically for Operation Torch. *USN photo*

Advanced Carrier Training Groups Pacific and Atlantic used new CVE-class carriers to train combat aircrews. SBD Dauntlesses are spotted in front of F6F Hellcats and TBF Avengers prior to launch from an escort carrier c. mid-1943. *USN photo*

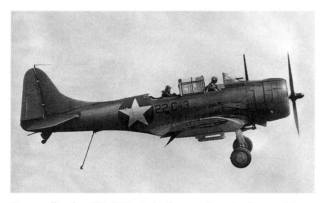

Externally, the 780 SBD-4s built were barely discernible from the -3s. They had a 24-volt electrical system, radar, and radio/navigation gear added. A VC-22 SBD-4 makes its approach to *Independence* (CVL-22) 1 May 1943. Squadron was in stateside training at the time; squadron designations were eliminated from fuselage markings prior to combat deployment. Practice bomb container is on starboard wing rack. *USN photo*

As new models of the Dauntless began reporting to the fleet, the SBD-1s went to the training command. A Naval Aviation Operational Training Command -1 in flight c. 1943. *USN photo*

month through the end of May. In Best's case, he logged just two flights during June: two launches, two bombs dropped, two Japanese carriers sunk, two arrested landings. Total time: 7.3 hours. His previous 2,737 flight hours and 328 "traps" had been well spent in preparation for Midway, the most important battle in the history of the U.S. Navy.

Meanwhile, the Douglas factory, overwhelmed with orders for scout-bombers that had been headed for obsolescence, struggled to keep vital parts coming from subcontractors. Items such as fuel valves and propellers were often in short supply during early 1942 until the "pipeline" caught up with demand. Production increased from an average of 20 Dauntlesses per month in late 1941

By mid-1944, the Dauntless was nearing the end of its service in carrier air groups. The last two navy squadrons to operate the SBD were VB-10 in *Enterprise* (CV-6) and VB-16 in *Lexington* (CV-16). VB-10 SBD-5s launch from CV-6 c. late 1943 or early 1944. *USN photo*

to 11 a day when the El Segundo plant kicked into high gear. The record for Dauntless production was set during May 1943 when 376 SBD-5s and A-24Bs were delivered.

The workhorse of the Pacific Theater throughout 1942 was the SBD-3, which was present at Coral Sea, dominated the Midway battle, and became the only dive-bomber of Guadalcanal's "Cactus Air Force." The best example of what the Dauntless meant to the war against Japan is that in the year following Pearl Harbor, Dauntlesses probably sank more combatant tonnage than the rest of the U.S. Navy combined.

Among the Dauntless warriors who flew the SBD was Lt. Comdr. W. J. "Gus" Widhelm of *Hornet's* Scouting Squadron Eight. He related, "The Dauntless is tough. It can take as well as give. You can't tear it

apart no matter what you do to it, and it will withstand incredible punishment."

Lt. Col. Richard C. Mangrum, commanding the first SBD squadron ashore on Guadalcanal, insisted, "The ruggedness of the SBD kept us in business. The Dauntless never let us down." He knew whereof he spoke: During the crucial phase of the campaign, portions of six navy and six whole marine SBD squadrons flew from Henderson Field for periods varying between a few days and several weeks. Among them, they constituted by far the greatest offensive weapon available to the Cactus Air Force. In contrast, three Avenger squadrons sent crews ashore during the Guadalcanal campaign.

SBD development continued for most of the war. Early dash threes lacked rubber-lined self-sealing fuel

In a fitting semi-finish, VB-10 and VB-16 Dauntlesses struck the Japanese Fleet off the Marianas during the Battle of the Philippine Sea, 19–20 June 1944. The SBD was the only U.S. Navy aircraft to fly from carriers in World War II's five carrier battles. VB-10, led by squadron CO, Lt.James D. "Jig Dog" Ramage, launches into the setting sun for the daring long-range mission. *USN photo*

A VB-16 SBD-5 returns to *Lexington* (CV-16) during the Marshalls/Gilbert campaign during November 1943. Although VB-16 was one of the last two SBD carrier squadrons, the honor of the last SBD combat from a carrier went to Jig Ramage's VB-10, when on 5 July 1944, the squadron attacked targets on Guam. *USN photo*

tanks, but wartime production soon remedied that fault and retrofit kits were sent to the fleet. In October 1942 the SBD-4 began production—identical to the dash three except for an upgraded electrical system. It phased out of production in April 1943.

The most numerous version, the SBD-5, appeared in February 1943 and accounted for fully half of all Dauntless production. Besides an upgraded Wright engine, the SBD-5 had an internally mounted reflector sight, thus avoiding the fogging problem common to aircraft in moist tropical atmosphere.

The final model, the "dash six," began production in February 1944. It had a 1,350-horsepower engine and more internal fuel than its predecessor, but only 450 were built. There was no USAAF version of the SBD-6.

Though the Curtiss Helldiver had largely replaced Douglas SBDs in the Fast Carrier Task Force by July, the two remaining fleet squadrons made a strong showing in the Battle of the Philippine Sea. Nearly all the Dauntlesses launched against the Japanese Mobile Fleet on 20 June returned safely to the task force while only a fraction of the Helldivers made the round trip. The two Dauntless squadron leaders—Lt. Comdrs. James D. Ramage of *Enterprise's* VB-10 and Ralph Weymouth of *Lexington's* VB-16—told Vice Adm. Marc Mitscher that they felt the SBD should be retained in favor of its Curtiss successor, but by then it was too late. The old warhorse was being put out to pasture.

Dauntless production ended in August 1944 with the last 16 SBD-6s, making a total of 5,936 SBDs and A-24s from El Segundo and Tulsa. By comparison, from 1939 to 1945 Junkers built 4,900 Ju-87 *Stukas* while Aichi and its subcontractor produced 1,500 D3A "Vals."

Among its numerous records and historical footnotes, the Dauntless remained the only American carrier aircraft of World War II designed and wholly produced without folding wings. Largely because of the fixed size of prewar carrier squadrons, 36 SBDs could be embarked in a *Lexington* (CV-2)- or *Yorktown* (CV-5)-class carrier without unduly crowding the flight deck, though Dauntlesses were more likely to remain "topside" than their folding-wing counterparts, which could be maintained on the hangar deck.

Despite the Dauntless' well-known status in the fleet, at least a few sailors assumed they could fold their wings. During the frantic night recovery off Saipan on 20

Another duty of the Dauntless was inshore patrol squadron ASW operations by land-based units off the Atlantic Coast in the Caribbean. These missions were flown by U.S. Navy and Marine Corps squadrons. This VMS-3 flight of SBD-5s is from MCAS Bourne Field, St. Thomas, Virgin Islands, during May 1944. The aircraft are in the standard Atlantic ASW paint scheme of World War II. *USN photo*

June 1944, a *Lexington* (CV-16) Dauntless was trapped aboard an *Independence*-class light carrier, the only available deck. Nearly out of fuel, the dive-bomber pilot gratefully accepted directions to a parking place forward among the Avengers and Hellcats. "Fold your wings!" shouted a plane director, justifiably concerned with maximizing the limited space available.

"This is an SBD," replied the aviator.

"Well, fold 'em anyway," came the retort.

Aboard *Enterprise* that same evening, drama rather than humor was evident. Lt. Cook Cleland of VB-16 finally got aboard after multiple passes at three other ships, landing with difficulty, owing to a 40-mm shell that destroyed much of one landing flap. Plane handlers, seeing the damage, moved in to push his Dauntless overboard and make room for planes still airborne. Cleland insisted that his pet Dauntless, "Old Number 39," remain aboard for repair. An argument ensued and

Some Dauntlesses were modified for special missions, such as this VU-7 SBD-3P BuNo 06523 off San Diego, c. 1943, on a photo mission. *USN photo, Art Melvin*

was only resolved when the pilot pointedly reached for his pistol.

The Marianas campaign was the Dauntless' last while flying from carriers. By that summer of 1944, SBDs had logged 1,190,000 operational flight hours, or one-quarter of the total for navy carrier air groups as well as Marine Corps squadrons. Considering that F4F Wildcats, F6F Hellcats, F4U Corsairs, TBD Devastators, TBF Avengers, and SB2C Helldivers all had flown combat in that period, the Dauntless' contribution was amazingly disproportionate.

THE BOMBING CIRCLE

The Dauntless unarguably remained the premier dive-bomber of the U.S. armed forces. Operational records maintained by the Fourth Marine Aircraft Wing in the

Douglas stepped-up production of the SBD by opening a new plant in Tulsa, Oklahoma, where -5s were built for the navy. Tulsa also produced 450 SBD-6s. The 168 SBD-3A, 170 SBD-4A, and 675 SBD-5As were all built for the AAF as the A-24, A-24A, and A-24B, respectively. *Douglas photo, courtesy Harry Gann*

VS-51 SBD-5s were land-based with Fleet Air Wing One at Tutuila, Samoa, for island defense. *USN photo*

Marine SBD-5s on flight line at Tarawa, in the Gilbert Islands, in November 1944 with a Grumman J2F Duck. Graves of two marines who died in the battle for the island are in the foreground. *USMC photo, WO R.L. Chapel*

The marines fought their Dauntlesses land-based across the Pacific to the Philippine Islands. At war's end, they were still bombing enemy garrisons in the Solomons. The last operational Dauntless faded into obscurity from an unnamed Pacific squadron 30 September 1945. Here, an SBD-6 is in flight c. late 1944 in the tricolor scheme that adorned most SBDs. *Douglas photo, courtesy Harry Gann*

An SBD-3 BuNo 4587, last assigned to CASU 5, lies on the ocean floor off San Diego in these late 1990s photos. There is high interest, especially with former SBD crewmen, in raising and restoring the Dauntless. *USN photos*

This close-up view of a VC-22 Douglas SBD-4 radioman/gunner well illustrates typical flight gear, armor plate, and red-tipped tracer rounds of the period, 30 April 1943. At the time, VC-22 was assigned to the light carrier *Independence* (CV-22), the name ship of her class. *Independence*-class CVs were redesignated CVL on 15 July 1943. *USN photo*

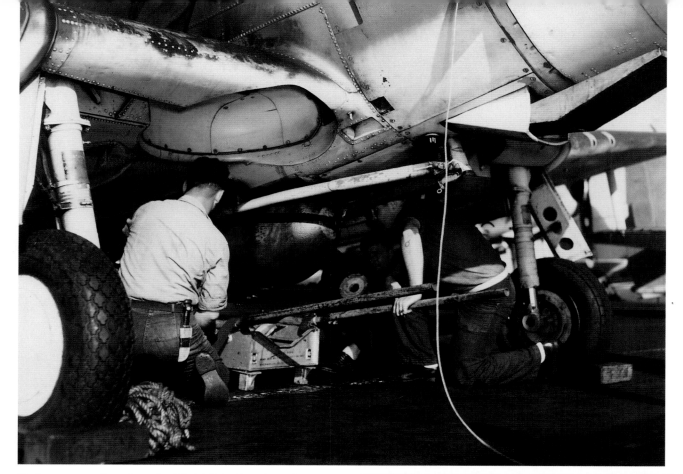

Ordnancemen "bomb up" a VB-16 SBD-5 on board *Lexington* (CV-16) for a late 1943 mission. *USN photo CDR Edw. Steichen*

Marshall Islands during 1944–1945 plotted the fall of almost every bomb delivered against bypassed Japanese garrisons. The bombing yardstick was called "circular error of probability" (CEP), expressed as a radial within which half the bombs struck. The wing's three SBD squadrons logged an overall CEP of 175 feet, meaning that 50 percent of Dauntless bombs landed within 175 feet of the target.

Naturally, the CEP was somewhat affected by the size of various targets. In the Marshalls they ranged from gun positions of 25 to 50 feet in diameter to buildings of 250 feet or so. Vought F4Us, also widely used as dive-bombers, performed commendably even by SBD standards with an average 195-foot CEP and near-identical direct hit ratios on the varied targets: from 5.4 percent on 50-foot targets for Dauntlesses to 4.5 percent for Corsairs. Against well-defended targets still capable of putting up flak, marine pilots increased their release altitude from 1,700 feet to 3,000 yet maintained most of their previous accuracy. On larger targets, Dauntless pilots scored three hits out of four bombs while Corsair pilots were two of three.

Advanced Carrier Training Group Pacific ordnanceman loads ammunition into an SBD's 30-caliber twin-mount on board a PacFlt CVE during training exercises off the West Coast. *USN photo*

FOREIGN CLIMES

The Dauntless family served in three foreign combat arms during the war: organizations as disparate as the French Air Force and navy as well as the New Zealand Air Force. Additionally, the tiny Mexican Air Force obtained A-24s before the end of hostilities.

One New Zealand squadron flew former U.S. Marine Corps Dauntlesses in the Southwest Pacific region.

Positioning and movement of aircraft on board carriers is a precision process planned and tracked in the aircraft handler's spaces located at the base of the island at flight deck level. Here, a *Randolph* (CV-15) crewman keeps aircraft positions up to date by use of made-to-scale templates on a metal board outline of the flight and hangar decks. *USN photo*

Number 25 Squadron, RNZAF, was established with SBD-3s in July 1943 and completed training with "dash fours" early the next year. When deployed to Bougainville Island in February 1944, "Number 25" was fully equipped with SBD-5s, which it flew against Rabaul, New Britain, during a two-month tour. Plans for a second Kiwi Dauntless squadron were abandoned when the Corsair's dive-bombing capability was proven.

Meanwhile, on the other side of the globe, Free French squadrons received A-24s in North Africa during 1943, and eventually amalgamated them into *Groupe de Combat I/18*. In the summer of 1944 the group deployed to southern France, joining American and British forces in driving the Germans out of areas they had occupied for four years.

Additionally, a French naval air group flew SBD-5s in France, beginning in late 1944. *Groupe Aeronavale 2* began operations in December, continuing until the German surrender five months later. After the war the landlocked Dauntlesses logged "traps" on two French light carriers until 1949, with other aircraft remaining in Morocco as late as 1953.

FLYING THE DAUNTLESS

From 1970 to 1974 the author had the pleasure of helping to restore the only airworthy Dauntless at that time. All too few hours were spent airborne in the A-24B,

ACTG Pac plane inspectors (identified by green jerseys and caps with black stripes) work on a Dauntless on board a CVE off the West Coast, c. mid-1943. *USN photo*

Largely unheralded, maintenance personnel have been the key to successful flight operations throughout the history of naval aviation. Without these individuals, the pilots and aircrew would never get off the ground to win the glory. An SBD-5 receives close attention c. 1943–1944. *USN photo*

which was finished as an SBD-5, but the recollection stirs the memory three decades later.

Accustomed to the occasionally unpleasant stall characteristics of the SNJ advanced trainer, a new dive-bomber pilot had an aircraft that landed at about the same airspeed as the "J-Bird" and possessed markedly easier ground-handling qualities. While the SNJ had noticeably better brakes, the SBD was, after all, designed as a carrier aircraft!

Visibility from the pilot's seat was good, though not outstanding due to the narrow windscreen. The cockpit was well planned and laid out, with most controls and knobs coming easily to hand. The gunner had an exceptionally fine view along the rear hemisphere due to his full-swivel seat and two canopy sections that slid forward out of the way.

The SBD-5s and -6s had flight and throttle controls in the rear cockpit, making it possible for the gunner to spell the pilot or at least to keep the plane under control in an emergency.

From a crew comfort perspective, the SBD received moderate grades. It was drafty, and engine noise could be fatiguing on long flights. However, both cockpits were roomy, though the radioman-gunner was, of course, enclosed in the ring mount for his twin .30 caliber guns.

On takeoff the SBD-5 had 1,200 horsepower available but did not require full throttle with a light load. The rudder trim tab handled most of the torque and the rudder itself was sufficient to keep the plane tracking straight down the runway. Acceleration was impressive with light takeoff weight, and the Wright Cyclone's staccato bark reminded me for all the world of a six-cylinder hot rod revving up. Fully fueled and bearing a useful ordnance load, however, the SBD was underpowered throughout its career. The one request from Dauntless pilots was "more power."

The Dauntless immediately came alive as a flying machine. All controls were responsive early in the takeoff roll, but the ailerons were especially outstanding. They were so light that it was possible to overcontrol the airplane in the first couple of flights. Beside being delightfully easy to handle, the ailerons also were remarkably efficient. The slightest stick movement brought a surprising degree of bank. The Dauntless was blessed with a roll rate that was considered good even by fighter standards—certainly a desirable quality for keeping a dive-bomber on target in a steep attack.

Depicting an era long gone by, this photo shows the workings of this SBD's Wright Cyclone R-1820 radial engine c. early 1944. The final reciprocal engine aircraft was phased out of the Navy in September 1988 when the last Grumman C-1A Trader COD was retired to the Naval Aviation Museum. Personnel in photo are Aviation Machinist Mate 1st class J. Phillips, atop engine; Aviation Machinist Mate 3rd class D. F. Peterson, at right; and Aviation Ordnanceman 3/c at left. *USN photo*

Stall characteristics were good by nearly any yardstick, and a pilot with any feel for the airplane would easily anticipate the break. The rudder was effective at low airspeed, as were the ailerons, and kept the SBD well in hand until the inevitable drop-off to port. Recovery was accomplished without difficulty from stalls and spins, provided some leeway was accorded to secondary stalls, which were not wholly unknown.

For all its docile and pleasant flight characteristics, the Dauntless was built for the purpose of putting a bomb precisely on target. The considerable dihedral of

New fighters and attack planes began replacing the prewar types in mid-1942. CVG-5 embarked in *Yorktown* (CV-10) was typical with Grumman F6F-3s and TBF-1s, along with Douglas SBD-Ss, during November–December 1943 raids on the Marshalls and Gilberts. *USN photo, Lt. Charles Kerlee, courtesy Doug Siegfried*

The Battle of Midway, 4–6 June 1942, turned the tide of war against the Japanese in the Pacific. The battle was won by the SBD dive bombers launched from three U.S. carriers. Much of the success of the battle was attributed to Lt. Comdr. Wade C. McCluskey, *Enterprise* CAG, who located the Japanese Fleet while flying an SBD. McCluskey, a fighter pilot, led his SBDs against the carrier *Kaga*, scoring a hit. He was wounded by Zeroes during the battle but safely returned to CV-6. *USN photo*

the SBD's wings made for a solid sighting platform, so essential to accuracy. The dive brakes, inherited from its Northrop predecessor, allowed the Dauntless to drop downhill at about 240 knots (c. 275 miles per hour). Standard push-over altitude was 15,000 feet, at which point the pilot slowed the airplane, pulled the nose above the horizon, and activated the combined landing flap/dive brake handle on his right-hand console. He then entered the dive, picking up the target as the nose settled on a 70-degree angle.

A dive from 15,000 feet took about 35 seconds, with a typical release altitude of 2,500 feet. Recovery required pulling at least 4 or 5 Gs, and the dive flaps had to be closed immediately after release because the airplane would not maintain level flight with the brakes extended.

The Dauntless was an easy aircraft to land aboard ship, within the rigorous confines of that esoteric art. The "letter box" stall slots in the leading edge of each wing helped reduce stall speed, but mostly they improved low-speed stability. Perhaps only the Grumman Hellcat rivaled the Dauntless as what some aviators called "a baby buggy" of a tailhook airplane.

Between them, the Dauntless and the Hellcat were significant partners in the demise of the Empire of the Sun.

Another SBD pilot at Midway was VB-3's commanding officer, Lt. Comdr. Max Leslie, who led a successful attack against the carrier *Soryu*. Although frustrated by a malfunctioning bomb-release switch, Leslie continued his attack by strafing the carrier, helping to protect his squadron mates as they pressed their attacks. He and his crewman were rescued after ditching from fuel starvation after the long-range attack. *USN photo, courtesy Rear Adm. Max Leslie, USN (Ret)*

RIGHT TOP:
Lt. Comdr. James D. "Jig Dog" (from the old phonetic alphabet for J and D) Ramage led VB-10 through some of the Pacific War's heaviest fighting, flying first with VS-10 from *Espiritu Santo* and then from *Enterprise* (CV-6). Ramage earned a Navy Cross at the Battle of the Philippine Sea in June 1944 and brought all 12 of his squadron's planes back to the task force after the "Mission in Darkness." *USN photo, courtesy Rear Adm. J. D. Ramage, USN (Ret)*

RIGHT:
Capt. Robert M. "Bob" Elder, USN (Ret), flew both SBCs and SBDs while serving as an ensign with VB-3 from *Saratoga* (CV-3). Elder flew Dauntlesses in the battles of Coral Sea, Midway, and Guadalcanal. At Midway, he assisted in sinking the Japanese carriers *Soryu* and *Hiryu*, as well as heavily damaging the heavy carrier *Mikuma*. Later, at Guadalcanal, he was credited with damaging the seaplane tender *Chitose*. He was awarded two Navy Crosses for his World War II actions in the Pacific. *USN photo, courtesy Capt. R. M. Elder, USN (Ret)*

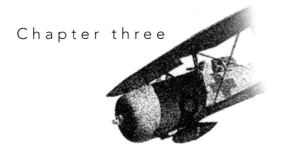

Chapter three

Curtiss SB2C
Helldiver

The Curtiss SB2C Helldiver story was one of institutional mood swings: from high expectation to bitter disappointment to grudging acceptance. Intended to replace the Douglas Dauntless by 1942, the SB2C lagged far behind schedule and never really caught up. By fortunate irony, the initial failure of Curtiss' problem-plagued dive-bomber may have saved a bitter American defeat at Guadalcanal, where the SBD's rugged simplicity kept the Cactus Air Force in business.

Curtiss-Wright Aeronautical Company was one of the world leaders in military aviation during the 1930s. Best known for a successful line of army fighters and navy dive-bombers, the Buffalo, New York, firm entered a competition for a new carrier-based scout-bomber in 1938. The XSB2C-1 was favored over four other entries, and such was the navy's confidence in the Curtiss that it ordered 370 in May 1939. It was an extraordinary step in any case, but all the more so because the "interim" scout-bomber, the Douglas Dauntless, was not yet in production.

However, the Bureau of Aeronautics' (BuAer's) optimism proved wholly unfounded, as the prototype SB2C would not fly for another year and a half. A partial redesign of the wing was necessary, as wind tunnel tests demonstrated a high stall speed that would have compromised carrier suitability. Then, after the prototype flew in December 1940, it encountered stability problems and the aircraft was damaged in a crash two months later when the R-2600 engine failed.

Despite the maddening problems, the company and the navy were committed to the aircraft, with a new factory opening at Columbus, Ohio, on 4 December 1941. That good news was offset by a wing failure 17 days later; the test pilot survived but the prototype was destroyed.

And so it went. Further flight tests revealed a decline in top speed and an increase in landing speed, with hundreds of minor changes required on each completed aircraft before delivery to the navy. Another facility was established at Columbus to

Commander Air Force Pacific ordered that by 1 March 1945 all PacFlt carrier aircraft would bear individual geometric pattern markings assigned to each carrier. VB-83 SB2C-4s and -4Es are off Okinawa in April 1945, wearing the pattern assigned to *Essex* (CV-9). *USN photo, courtesy Paul Madden*

Intended to replace the SBD by 1942, the SB2C lagged far behind schedule, plagued by structural problems. VB-17 took the "Beast" aboard *Bunker Hill* (CV-17) in July 1943 for a shakedown cruise. The SB2C Helldiver's performance was so poor that CV-17's skipper, Capt. J. J. "Jocko" Clark, recommended cancellation of the new dive-bomber. VB-17 SB2C-1 loses its tail feathers during landing on board *Bunker Hill* 17 July 1943. *USN photo*

modify the "completed" Helldivers as they came off the production line.

The original recipient of production SB2C-1 Helldivers was Scouting Squadron Nine in April 1942. A myriad of problems dogged the Curtiss bomber, however, and the first two carriers that received the type converted to Dauntlesses. *Essex* (CV-9) and *Yorktown* (CV-10)

lacked the time to "shake out" the Helldivers, and in fact *Yorktown's* commanding officer, Capt. J. J. Clark, recommended against procuring further Helldivers. Problems as diverse as hook skip, collapsed landing gear, and structural failures cast a cloud over the entire program.

The first SB2C combat unit was VB-17, one of the "plankowner" squadrons in USS *Bunker Hill* (CV-17),

The SB2C-1 Helldiver's initial carrier operation problems were as diverse as hook skip, collapsed landing gear, and structural failures. *Yorktown* (CV-10) flight deck crewmen rush to aid an SB2C-1 that collapsed a tail wheel on landing in May 1943. *USN photo*

The follow-on SB2C-3 production model (the XSB2C-2 was a floatplane test project) had a 1,900 horsepower Wright R-2600-20 engine with 200 more horsepower than the -2's 2600-8. Even so, usually overloaded and still underpowered, many "Deuce" pilots went into the drink, especially if they were first to launch with a limited deck run. VB-82 pilot Lt. O. R. Brown abandons his -3 after crashing off *Charger* (CVE-30) 21 June 1944. *USN photo*

which initiated "The Beast" to combat in November 1943. From that point, another eight months would pass before Helldivers fully replaced Dauntlesses aboard the fast carriers.

As a weapon, the SB2C-1 left much to be desired. Despite its lengthy gestation, the "Beast" entered fleet service as a marginal dive-bomber, owing to buffeting caused by the original dive flaps' irregular slipstream over the empennage. Additionally, its relatively heavy controls made precise corrections more difficult in a dive—a problem of major concern to pilots weaned on the SBD's beautifully balanced ailerons.

Meanwhile, additional Helldiver production was arranged north of the border, where Canadian Car and Foundry and Fairchild Canada produced the SBW and SBF, respectively. The two companies delivered 1,134 aircraft, some of which flew side by side in combat with Curtiss-built machines. More SBW-3s and SBF-3s were manufactured than the other Canadian models combined.

Helldiver production increased dramatically from 1943 onward: Curtiss and the Canadian factories delivered 627 SB2Cs, SBFs, and SBWs that year but tripled the output in 1944 with a total of 3,319. During 1945 another 2,018 were produced, with Canadian production ending in August and Curtiss deliveries in October.

Armament in the Helldiver series was a perennial problem for the first year or more. Though designed

Entering combat at Rabaul in November 1943 with VB-17, the SB2C began replacing SBDs in the fleet, completing the transition eight months later to become the Navy's mainstay dive-bomber. VB-80 SB2C-4 Helldivers flying from *Hancock* (CV-19) en route to their targets during D-Day for the Iwo Jima campaign 19 February 1945. *USN photo*

Construction of the SB2C was farmed out to two Canadian aircraft factories and redesignated. SBWs were built by Canadian Car and Foundry, while SBFs were produced by Fairchild Canada. VB-11 SBW-3 returns to *Hornet* (CV-12) following a mission in late 1944. *USN photo*

SB2Cs were produced in several versions, the most numerous of which was the SB2C-4; 2,045 of them were built. This -4 was used only June–September 1943. *USN photo*

with two .30-caliber machine guns firing through the propeller arc, the first 200 "dash one" models were delivered with four wing-mounted .50 calibers. Fleet experience led to replacement of the .50s with two 20-mm cannons, which provided greater striking power but suffered occasional malfunctions.

Initially the radioman-gunner was to operate a powered turret similar to that in the Grumman Avenger. However, the two .50 calibers envisioned for the rear-seat man eventually gave way to the standard twin .30 mount common to most versions of the Dauntless. A residual problem arose in the Canadian-built SBW model, as hydraulic lines intended for the turret were retained on the production line and caused frequent leaks.

An ordnance alternative in the SB2C was provision for a 2,000-pound torpedo, mounted on fuselage bomb racks and the bomb displacing gear fittings on the firewall. The torpedo option was never needed, but the fact that it was built into the Helldiver proved the BuAer's continuing design philosophy toward a generic

SB2C-4Es were modifications of the basic -4 and normally carried an APS-4 radar pod under the starboard wing. Later -4s had four rocket launcher rails under each wing. VB-35 -4E flying from *Shangri-La* (CV-38) is on a photo mission 17 August 45. It has the rocket rails but no radar pod. *USN photo*

attack aircraft, dating from 1941. With adequate fighters available for strike escort by 1943, the "torpecker" role might have been assigned to bombing squadrons, but the division of labor remained unchanged throughout the balance of the war.

Two 325-pound depth charges could be carried in the internal bomb bay, but SB2C Helldivers were seldom required in the antisubmarine role and it is unlikely that SB2Cs made any attacks on Axis subs.

Four zero-length rocket rails were added under each wing of the SB2C-3, though Helldivers flew relatively few sorties with HVARs, accounting for only 2 percent of the total fired by carrier aircraft. On the other hand, the Curtiss bombers logged more than 4,800 combat sorties against Japanese ships—merchant and combatant—which was three times as many as the SBD. Overall, regardless of the types of targets, SB2Cs dropped nearly 11,000 tons of bombs in the Pacific War compared to 2,500 tons by carrier-based Dauntlesses. Clearly, the Helldiver paid its way on the long saltwater trail to

Tokyo Bay, but it seldom achieved the devoted following that pilots readily accorded the Dauntless.

GROWING PAINS

Pilots vividly recall the problems involved in transitioning from SBDs to Helldivers, both because of the technical difficulties and the limited time available.

Bombing Squadron Eight had only about a month in fall 1943 to make the transition—to say nothing of carrier qualifications. Recalled Rear Adm. Martin Carmody, then a senior lieutenant, "The first two days of CarQuals aboard the newly launched *Intrepid* (CV-11) was a fiasco for VB-8, mainly because our pilots did not have enough experience in the 'Beast.' After two aircraft went into the water on takeoff, due to engine trouble, the decision was made to send our squadron to Xeris Field on Trinidad for additional Field Carrier Landing Practice and engine maintenance."

Eventually Bombing Eight deployed to combat in *Bunker Hill*, relieving VB-17, the original Helldiver squadron.

Even in peacetime, carrier operations are hazardous; wartime only increases the risks to carrier air crews. VB-85 SB2C-4E BuNo 20543 was demolished after it struck and somersaulted over the flight deck barricade on board *Shangri-La* (CV-38) 3 February 1945. The rear gunner still strapped to his gun mount seat has been thrown from the aircraft while the pilot is trapped inside. *USN photo*

Curtiss built 900 Helldivers for the U.S. Army Air Forces. Many of these aircraft, designated A-25A Shrike, were reassigned to the Marine Corps and were used land-based as SB2C-1A Helldivers. All but the first 10 of these planes had no wing-fold capability, none had arresting hooks. USAAF A-25A "Torchy Tess" is shown in a Curtiss publicity photo c. 1943. *Curtiss photo, courtesy Hal Andrews*

A similar case was Bombing Squadron Three. A distinguished Dauntless unit with enemy carriers to its credit at Midway and Guadalcanal, VB-3 turned in its new SBD-5s for SB2C-1C at NAS Whidbey Island in November 1943. Curtiss was slow to deliver the full complement of aircraft, and those that did arrive still required post-production modifications. Consequently, the squadron's training syllabus was adversely affected.

Though pilots relished the speed of their new mounts, problems remained for several months. When the tired -1Cs were turned over to the fleet pool in Hawaii during July 1944, any elation was short-lived. Bombing Three received 36 SBW-3s that unaccountably had not received as many post-production alterations as the initial batch of SB2Cs. More valuable training time was lost because the Canadian Car and Foundry aircraft were prohibited from conducting bombing and gunnery flights.

Canadian Car and Foundry built 26 SBW-1Bs for Great Britain under the Lend-Lease program. Following World War II, Helldivers also served with French, Greek, Italian, Portuguese, and Thai forces. *USN photo*

An SB2C-1C, assigned to Advanced Carrier Training Group Pacific, shows the position of a 20mm cannon mounted in each wing, as well as the leading edge flaps that assisted the big bomber in slow speed regimens. "Yaggi" radar antenna under the port wing is also visible, a characteristic of -1Cs and later versions, until the APS-4 radar pod was developed. *USN photo*

War-weary SB2Cs rest at an aircraft pool on NAS Ford Island, T.H., 27 March 1945. *USN photo*

Subsequently, more SB2C-1Cs were issued to VB-3 specifically for carrier qualification. The last SBWs were detached in October, and the Panther squadron gratefully received two dozen new SB2C-4s prior to deploying in *Yorktown* (CV-10), namesake of the ship that VB-3 had ridden to glory at Midway two and a half years previously.

Personnel on carrier squadrons that had trained with Dauntlesses were often reluctant to change to Helldivers, an attitude only reinforced by the debacle off Saipan in June 1944. Fuel exhaustion was the main cause of 90 percent losses, but enemy action and deck crashes also took their toll.

During the "mission beyond darkness" of 20 June 1944, 52 Helldivers were launched against the beaten Japanese carrier force. Those SB2Cs that survived flak and fighters largely succumbed to fuel exhaustion, as related by Lt. (jg) Dominic Scatuorchio of USS *Wasp's* VB-14:

"When I definitely knew I had to make a water landing, I informed my gunner to get ready. He remained very calm, tightened his safety belt and shoulder harness,

got the rubber raft out, laid it across the gunner's ring, and locked the hood open.

"With five gallons of gas, I headed east, tightened my safety belt and shoulder harness, locked the hood back, but did not take off my chute. At 600 feet I dropped my flaps, slowed to 70 knots, kept my wings level with the gyro horizon, and controlled my rate of descent with the throttle at 250 feet per minute.

"When I hit the water, the shock was about the same as a carrier landing. I disconnected my safety belt, got out on the wing, but was jerked back by my phone cord. I paused to disconnect it, yelled to my gunner, got an 'O.K.,' and then reached in and got one canteen out. My gunner got the raft and emergency kit out, but we didn't inflate the raft immediately as the tail of the plane was right above us. The plane finally sank nose down after about two and one-half minutes. At the time of its sinking, I was only about three feet from the plane, but felt no suction. We inflated the raft and climbed aboard.

The SB2C remained in fleet service until VA-54 retired its last SB2C-5 by 1 June 1949. The "Deuce" remained with the reserves until the early 1950s. A total of 7,139 Helldivers were built for the U.S. Navy, Air Force, and several foreign countries. A VA-9A SB2C-5 is brought up *Philippine Sea's* (CV-47) aft elevator for launch during Air Group 9's 1948 Med cruise. *John Moore*

Maintaining a carrier's catapult and arresting gear is a full-time job for flight deck crews. The continual strain and wear on the equipment from the loads imposed by heavy aircraft requires a constant vigilance by carrier personnel. ACTG Pac CVE arresting gear crew works on a fiddle bridge, designed to raise cross-deck pendants off the deck to enable the aircraft tailhook to engage the wire. *USN photo*

ACTG Pac CVE barrier operator checks the "last resort" wire barrier for proper operation prior to flight operations. The barrier is raised during landing operations to prevent any aircraft that misses all of the arresting wires from crashing into personnel and/or equipment forward of the landing area. *USN photo*

Arresting gear personnel perform maintenance on an ACTG Pac CVE's wire barrier. The weapon at base of island is a practice Mk. 13 aerial torpedo, painted yellow to identify it as training ordnance—containing no explosives. *USN photo*

"The above action occurred at 2010 on 20 June. No planes were spotted on the 21st, but at 0800 on 22 June we saw two planes and let go a smoke bomb, attracting an F6F. At about 1130 a ship appeared on the horizon; I signaled with my mirror and the (destroyer) *Miller* changed course and picked us up at 1241 in position latitude 14-18N, longitude 137-00E."

When the tallies were all in, the 52 Helldivers on this mission had sustained catastrophic losses. Thirty-five had ditched, four were shot down and four more crashed trying to get aboard a carrier. Of the remaining nine, only two returned to their own ship. However, efficient search and rescue work limited SB2C personnel losses to 8 pilots and 10 air crewmen.

Though bitterly disappointed in the Helldiver, fleet squadrons had no option but to make the best of the situation. Dauntless production was just weeks from termination, without adequate spare parts in the pipeline.

Fortunately, the latest Helldiver model was available before the Battle of Leyte Gulf four months later. By October 1944, all eight dive-bomber squadrons of the Fast Carrier Task Force had received SB2C-3 or radar-equipped -3Es in time for the largest naval engagement of the war, and the improvements were badly needed.

Probably the most important step accomplished in the manufacture of the "dash three" was simplifying the complex hydraulic system, thus easing The Beast's perennial maintenance problems.

The SB2C also was a burden on flight deck crews, who found it difficult to move or to fit into some of the confined spaces aboard ship. The factory had taken heed of complaints from the fleet and addressed some of the most serious faults by simplifying the hydraulic system and providing a more powerful R-2600 with a four-bladed Curtiss electric propeller. The "dash four" Helldiver, with aerodynamically improved dive flaps, was available in increasing numbers before the first Tokyo strikes in February 1945. Offensive potential also was increased with the addition of underwing rocket rails. The final variant, the SB2C-5, entered service in summer 1945, benefiting primarily from greater internal fuel capacity, but evidently was not used in combat.

Despite its long-term problems, the Helldiver had its supporters. Once the early structural problems were solved, the dash one Beast stood up well to the rigors of carrier landings, and its rugged airframe could survive battle damage that might have destroyed lesser aircraft. The original four wing-mounted .50-caliber machine guns gave way to a pair of 20-mm cannons, which were endorsed by bomber pilots who appreciated the potential for strafing or air-to-air combat. Throughout a 20-month Pacific War career, SB2C squadrons reported engaging at least 82 Japanese aircraft, of which 44 were credited as shot down by Helldiver pilots and gunners. In exchange, some 17 Beasts were known lost to enemy aircraft. The low rate of enemy interception was, of course, testimony to the work of carrier-based F6F and F4U fighters.

A *Lexington* aviator, Lt. (jg) William S. Emerson, recounted the experience level typical of many dive-bomber pilots. "Just for fun, I added up how experienced I was in the 'Monster' when I went on my first combat flight. Ye olde logbook says when I launched, as part of the squadron's first combat strike on 18 July 1944, I had 95.5 hours, 7 carrier landings, and 1 catapult shot in the Helldiver. We felt pretty good about the SB2C-3, particularly after having experienced the -1 and -1C. That four-bladed prop and 200 extra horses made a big difference."

From the SB2C-3 onward, air crews became more confident in their mount. Able to make steeper, faster dives with heavy-g pullouts, their exposure to enemy flak was reduced proportionately.

Helldiver construction ended in October 1945, the month after Japan's formal surrender, with a grand total of 7,139 aircraft, of which the parent factory produced 5,105, or nearly three-quarters.

No foreign air arms adopted the Helldiver during World War II, though the U.S. Army and Marine Corps both used the type, and some would claim that only the army is more "foreign" to the navy than the marines! Some 900 Helldivers with nonfolding wings were designated A-25 Shrikes, built at St. Louis, Missouri, and originally intended for the Army Air Forces. By the end of 1943, however, the USAAF had no further requirement for a dedicated dive-bomber, and most A-25s went to marine training squadrons in the United States. In "leatherneck" use, the Shrikes were redesignated SB2C-1A Helldivers, and eventually 25 marine squadrons operated them, including five land-based combat units in the Marshalls and Philippines. Combat losses amounted to 18 SB2C/SBW-3s and -4s between November 1944 and August 1945—an average of two per month.

Postwar foreign use included France, Greece, Italy, Portugal, and Thailand. But the Helldiver disappeared from U.S. Navy rolls in 1949, still remembered (fondly or otherwise) as "The Beast."

Different-colored jerseys identify flight deck personnel assignments, such as green: catapult/arresting gear crews, as well as support personnel such as photographers and aircraft technicians; red: emergency personnel; blue: plane handlers; brown: plane captains; and yellow: flight deck directors. A CV-16 gasoline crew relaxes between flight operations during November 1943. *USN photo, CDR Edw. Steichen*

Air Group 75, assigned to the new *Franklin D. Roosevelt* (CVB-42), was not formed soon enough to make it into combat. VT-75 SB2C-5 Helldivers are at Leeward Field, Guantanamo Bay, Cuba, during 1946 work-ups. *Captain Don W. Monson, USN (Ret)*

Chapter four

Douglas TBD Devastator

One of history's most maligned aircraft, the TBD Devastator was no devastator of the Empire of the Sun, but neither was it the "suicide coffin" it has been proclaimed to be. In fact, it was a progressive design when it became the first carrier monoplane to enter American service in 1937.

The U.S. Navy Bureau of Aeronautics recognized that the global trend in military aircraft was toward monoplanes. When bids were accepted for a new torpedo plane in 1934, however, only one of the three contenders was seriously considered. Great Lakes submitted a conventional biplane and while Hall proposed a monoplane, it was disregarded owing to its floatplane configuration. That left Douglas, whose XTBD-1 was easily the winner of the competition.

The Douglas design included some seemingly halfway measures that actually made sense. The semi-retractable landing gear was intended to provide at least minimal cushion for the airframe in case of a wheels-up landing, even though other naval aircraft had fully retractable gear at the time. Similarly, the torpedo was only partially enclosed within the belly of the aircraft, the nose portion being exposed at a 10-degree downward angle. The latter provision was included as a means of ensuring nose-first entry into the water to minimize any tendency to "porpoise" and broach the surface, which could result in an erratic run.

First flown in April 1935, the TBD was warmly greeted as a replacement for lumbering relics such as the Great Lakes TGs and Martin T4Ms. If for no other reason, the TBD—optimistically named "Devastator" by the joint army-navy committee in October 1941—was guaranteed a place in history by replacing fabric-covered biplanes aboard American aircraft carriers. The prototype passed its carrier qualification trials aboard *Lexington* and prepared to join the fleet.

The transition from biplanes to monoplanes required a period of adjustment in carrier air groups. Oper-

Enterprise's LSO guides a VT-6 Devastator back aboard c. July 1941 for workup training. VT-6 launched the first combat aerial torpedo attack in U.S. Navy history when, on 1 February 1942, they attacked ships at Kwajalein Atoll from CV-6. *USN photo*

First flown 15 April 1935, Douglas' TBD-1 Devastator was the U.S. Navy's first all-metal, low-wing carrier monoplane. It had a crew of three and carried a 2,000-pound torpedo, or bombs. The Devastator was also the first carrier plane to have hydraulically folding wings. BuNo 0268, the first production TBD-1, performs an experimental torpedo drop at NAS Hampton Roads, Virginia, 23 July 1937, while assigned to the experimental unit there. *USN photo, courtesy Harry Gann*

Oahu-based maneuvers of the Pacific Fleet of the late 1930s and early 1940s, which often featured defense of the Hawaiian Islands, were ironic in view of the success of the Japanese attack 7 December 1941. Torpedo 6 TBD-1s in formation off Diamond Head, Oahu, T.H., c. 1939. *USN photo*

The crew of 6-T-14 hastily scrambles up safety lines cast to them by *Enterprise's* (CV-6) flight deck crew after the aircraft went over the side upon landing, 4 September 1940. TBDs carried a crew of three: pilot, second pilot/bombardier (usually an enlisted pilot), and a rear radioman/gunner. *USN photo*

ating doctrine had to be modified to accommodate the technical and tactical differences among the Douglas torpedo planes, Curtiss bombers, Vought scouts, and Grumman fighters. Carrier aviators soon grew accustomed to "modern" aircraft, however, as the Vought SB2U and Northrop BT scout-bombers closely followed the TBD into service. The navy's first monoplane fighters, Brewster F2As, arrived in 1939.

Production Devastators closely resembled the prototype, except for a change to the canopy and 100 more horsepower in the dependable Pratt & Whitney R-1830 radial engine. Deliveries to the fleet began in August 1937, running through October 1939, by which time total production amounted to only 130 airframes. Of those, 100 remained by December 1941. The type fully equipped five TorpRons in the Pacific Fleet during the

Ranger (CV-4) was the last of the prewar carriers in commission when the TBD Devastator reached the fleet to receive the new torpedo bomber. Lack of torpedo storage capability caused the delay. Here, *Ranger's* VS-42 42-S-16 is off the East Coast c. 1941, flown by Lt. J. G. Bolt with Aviation Machinist Mate 3rd class Russell B. Pietz in the rear seat and AMM 3/c Kelly in the bombardier position. *Rudy Arnold, courtesy NASM*

first half of 1942 (*Lexington, Saratoga, Enterprise, Yorktown,* and *Hornet*) plus smaller units aboard *Ranger* and *Wasp* in the Atlantic Fleet. The original TBD recipient was *Saratoga's* Torpedo Squadron Three at NAS San Diego, California, and VT-3 would figure prominently in the history of the Douglas "torpecker."

An enlisted pilot, Wilhelm G. Esders, reported to VT-3 in 1938 and was enthralled with the big, shiny monoplanes. He thought the TBD "the most beautiful aircraft I had ever seen." Once he was qualified in the type, he became even more enthusiastic: "After a few hours in the TBD I was sure it was the best plane the navy had at that time. It was faster than anything I had flown, and I was in love with the aircraft. Soon field carrier landing practice took place, followed by carrier qualifications day and night. I was quite tense during my first landings, but found that, like the other pilots, I too could land on the carrier. During night CarQuals I never felt really at ease, and felt that way throughout my carrier life. I realized that many other pilots felt the same way.

"One of the early lessons that the LSO stressed was: don't ever let your aircraft get slow during final approach to a carrier, as the TBD did not have as much power as needed to make a rapid recovery. Returning to the ship with a torpedo or maximum bomb load, it was wise to drop the ordnance, for getting slow in the groove just

wasn't acceptable. After observing an aircraft hit the ramp, this wise counsel certainly made a lasting impression on the pilot."

Bill Esders remained with Torpedo Three more than four years and survived the Battle of Midway—no easy task in a Devastator.

Compared to previous torpedo planes, the TBD was extraordinarily complex. Some squadrons reported that pilots considered the checklist "impossibly long" and a few had difficulty mastering the big Douglas' hydraulic and electrical systems. However, operational losses were avoided until the second half of 1938 when eight planes were written off in collisions, deck crashes, and one case of unlocked wings before takeoff.

By 1942 the TBD clearly had lost its leading-edge status as a technological landmark. Less than five years in the fleet, it was an obsolescent aircraft in comparison to what the Japanese were flying. Nakajima's B5N, later code-named Kate, also had entered production in 1937 but was 25 knots faster than the Douglas and possessed greater range. Beyond that, the Japanese Navy had the finest aerial torpedo in the world. The Type 91 Model 2 was capable of 40 knots, and could be released at an astonishing 260 knots airspeed. By comparison, the American Mark 13, though packing a larger warhead, was a 33-knot weapon that had to be dropped at no

The Devastator's combat debut came 10 December 1941 when *Lexington* (CV-2) launched two VT-2 TBD-1s on an ASW mission against a Japanese I-class boat caught on the surface off Johnston Island, southwest of Oahu. They dropped depth charges that landed close aboard, but no damage was observed. This VT-6 TBD-1 is on a mission against Wake Island 24 February 1942. *USN photo*

TBD-1s had a Pratt & Whitney R-1830-64 850-horsepower engine and a top speed of 198 miles per hour at 8,000 feet, configured with a torpedo. This 6-T-13 is over the Hawaiian area during 1941. *USN photo, courtesy Steve Ewing*

more than 110 knots from only 50 feet. Thus, Imperial Navy air crews had far greater tactical flexibility in weapons employment.

U.S. Navy torpedo squadrons incurred another deficit in the final years of peace. Fleet doctrine stressed bombing rather than torpedo delivery, and some pilots went entire calendar years without dropping a practice "fish." Various formations were tested in an effort to improve the concentration of bomb patterns, but without notable success. The challenge of hitting a maneuvering ship by level bombing remained beyond the capability of most of the world's air arms, even with the American advantage of the fabled Norden sight in army and navy aircraft.

A senior TBD pilot was Lt. Robert Laub of *Enterprise's* Torpedo Squadron Six. The late Rear Admiral Laub recalled the Devastator in the 1970s, saying, "The XTBD may have flown at 200 knots, but I never flew an operational type that did better than 150 and that was downhill, with all the right conditions. You were doing well to make 120 knots in the TBD with a torpedo, and since the protruding 'fish' didn't create a great deal of drag, 130 knots clean was normal. The TBD took all day to climb to altitude and if you went to 15,000 feet in it, you just about used up all your fuel. Twelve thousand feet was maximum bombing altitude, and because we never went higher, we carried no oxygen—although the aircraft was equipped to handle it.

"The TBD-1 was very stable and easy to handle. It broke from the deck at 70 knots and landed with full flaps at 60, even though the flaps didn't change its handling characteristics much. It had a good, solid feel and was rock steady when coming aboard. The maneuvers we did with it were very limited. Basically the TBD-1 was a straight and level airplane. It would perform moderately sharp turns, but I wouldn't roll or spin it. Its glide ratio was rather short and although we thought it was modern in 1937, it was obsolete by 1942 and we knew it."

DEVASTATORS AT WAR

In early combat, the Pacific Fleet torpedo squadrons fought their equipment as well as the Japanese. Torpedo Six conducted the first aerial torpedo attack in U.S. Navy history when *Enterprise* launched a 1 February strike against Kwajalein Atoll. Simultaneously *Yorktown* attacked Japanese bases in the Gilbert Islands, losing four Devastators to weather and navigation problems. Damage to the enemy was relatively light in both operations.

In late February VT-6 bombed Wake Island, gaining marginal results. But on 10 March *Lexington* and *Yorktown* launched an ambitious combined attack against the Japanese naval-air complex at Lae, New Guinea. Torpedo Two loaded torpedoes and TorpRon Five had bombs, between them sinking one transport and damag-

Pacific Fleet carriers began a series of hit-and-run raids against Japanese land forces in the Marshalls and Gilberts during early 1942. Pictured are *Enterprise* Air Group SBDs and TBDs positioned for launch, 4 May 1942. *Enterprise* (CV-6) and *Hornet* (CV-8), units of Admiral Halsey's Task Force 16, were en route to the South Pacific following their successful Tokyo raid in April. *USN photo*

ing a tender. The *Lexington* TBDs might have inflicted greater damage except for malfunctioning torpedoes.

The next operation was a prelude to the Battle of the Coral Sea. On 4 May *Yorktown's* VT-5 launched two strikes against Tulagi, an anchorage north of Guadalcanal in the Solomon Islands, but was plagued by more maddening failures. From 23 sorties, only one hit was confirmed, resulting in a destroyer beaching itself.

Three days later VT-2 and -5 participated in the first battle between aircraft carriers. Operating in the Coral Sea, *Lexington* and *Yorktown* launched a coordinated bombing and torpedo attack that sank the light carrier *Shoho* with no casualties to the TBDs. It was by far the most successful Devastator operation of the war, partly because two air groups overwhelmed the enemy's defenses and partly because for the first and only time in 1942, a set-piece attack was initiated that duplicated peacetime training exercises.

The battle resumed the next day, 8 May, in unfavorable weather over the Japanese task force. Torpedo Two found the large carrier *Shokaku* and launched an unsuccessful attack, surviving determined fighter opposition and losing one crew to fuel exhaustion. Later that day the Japanese air groups retaliated, hitting both American flattops and mortally wounding *Lexington*. She sank that evening with 12 Devastators still aboard.

In its after-action report, Torpedo Two noted several observations and made a similar number of recommendations for future actions. Based on Coral Sea experience, other Pacific Fleet TorpRons could expect:

(A) That the enemy ship formation will be widespread;

(B) That the point of piercing the enemy screen should be chosen to reduce exposure to antiaircraft fire to a minimum;

(C) That fighter opposition is to be expected;

(D) That enemy fighters would have time for only one pass during the Devastators' approach to the target;

(E) That torpedo planes should scatter after the attack and fly at low level to the rendezvous point, which should be about 20 miles in the direction of "Point Option";

Rare color photos of Torpedo 8 Devastators depict flight operations on board *Hornet* (CV-8) just prior to the Battle of Midway. The upper photo shows Lt. (jg) Jeff Woodson and gunner Aviation Radioman 2nd class Otway Creasy, Jr., taxiing T-5 into launch position. Below: Ens. W. W. Abercrombie and Aviation Radioman 2nd class B. P. Phelps launch a T-13 armed with Mk. 13 aerial torpedo. *USN photos, courtesy Mark Horan*

Torpedo 8 pilots pose for a group photo on board *Hornet* (CV-8) just prior to the Battle of Midway. VT-8 skipper, Lt. Comdr. John C. Waldron, is third from right in the back row. Ens. George Gay is fourth from left in the front row. *USN photo, courtesy Mark Horan*

(F) That Japanese AA fire is accurate in fuze setting (range) but "weak in train" (deflection), resulting in flak bursts astern of a torpedo squadron passing 90 degrees to the ship;

(G) That a quartering, overtaking torpedo on the inside of the target vessel's turn is the ideal drop point for the formation leader.

VT-2 recommended the following:

(A) TBDs should not be launched more than 160 nautical miles from the expected contact point. If opposition was expected, maximum launch range should be 150, as unexpected delays or weather could extend the outbound leg.

(B) The "anvil" or "split" attack should be employed regardless of the direction of approach. The enemy carrier will begin turning when the first bombs are released, allowing the Devastators to take position on each side of the target.

(C) An approach altitude of 4,000 to 6,000 feet should be used, assuming position can be gained before enemy fighters intercept the squadron.

(D) Jinking would be necessary during the approach and withdrawal to minimize effectiveness of enemy AA fire.

Generally, VT-2's observations proved valid, but there was one major exception: The Coral Sea experience of minimum time for Zeroes to intercept was grossly optimistic, based solely on the isolated situation of 8 May when weather affected both Americans and Japanese.

FATEFUL MIDWAY

Only four weeks after Coral Sea, three TorpRons fought the most important naval battle of the war. *Enterprise*, *Hornet*, and *Yorktown* opposed four veteran Japanese carriers supporting the attempted seizure of Midway, only 1,100 miles from Honolulu. The Big E's VT-6 was the only combat veteran of the three, but *Saratoga's* displaced VT-3, hastily assigned to *Yorktown*, had a high order of air crew experience. Torpedo Eight was as new as the rest of *Hornet* Air Group. Taking the Coral Sea lessons to heart, improved defensive armament was installed in *Enterprise* and *Hornet* TBDs with twin .30 caliber mounts for the radioman-gunner. Though there was insufficient time to replace the original single mounts in VT-3 aircraft, the modifications made no significant difference.

On the morning of 4 June, the TBD's six-month perfect record came to a shattering end. Although no Devastators had been lost to enemy flak or fighters since the war began, on this date the torpedo bombers were chopped up piecemeal.

The day began poorly for the TorpRons and went downhill from there. For reasons still not known, *Hornet* launched its short-ranged aircraft first, a decision that put all 10 Wildcats in the water with fuel exhaustion. By the time Lt. Comdr. John Waldron's VT-8 got airborne, more time had passed, and the entire air group was already watching its fuel gauges. *Hornet's* SBDs flew 250 miles westbound, turned around and returned to the task force or to Midway. Waldron, with a superior sense of direction, took his 15 Devastators southwesterly and found the enemy carriers. Lacking fighter cover, VT-8 attacked unescorted and was destroyed in the process. Ironically, and unknown to the TBD crews, TorpRon Eight's six new TBF-1 Avengers based on Midway had preceded the TBDs, losing five aircraft.

Enterprise's VT-6 was next on the scene, also minus escorting Wildcats. Low clouds had obscured the Task Force 16 formations, prompting Fighting Six to lose track of its Devastators. However, Lt. Comdr. Eugene Lindsey led 14 TBDs against the Japanese Fleet and turned in to attack. Like Waldron, he died at the head of his squadron.

Finally, Lt. Comdr. Lance Massey arrived with a dozen aircraft of his Torpedo Three. *Yorktown's* was the only air group to manage a coordinated attack, though the half-dozen Wildcats were swamped by Zeroes of the Japanese combat air patrol. None of VT-3's planes got back to their ship, which was damaged in *Hiryu's* retaliatory strike. Two TBDs ditched near the U.S. task force with two pilots and one gunner eventually retrieved.

Of 41 Devastators launched, only four returned—all to *Enterprise*—and two of those were jettisoned with heavy damage. The reason for the carnage was as much tactical as technical: swarmed by large numbers of Zeroes, two of the TorpRons attacked independently without fighter escort or support of dive-bombers.

However, the appalling losses among the "torpeckers" set up the Japanese for a knockout blow. With enemy fighters and lookouts focused on the TBD squadrons' low-level approach, the aerial highway was clear for the

Although touted as the lone survivor of VT-8 at Midway, Ens. George Gay was not the only VT-8 pilot to survive the battle. Gay (second from right) was the lone survivor of the TBD contingent of VT-8 that launched from *Hornet* (CV-8). VT-8 pilot Ens. Bert Earnest, flying a TBF-1 from Midway, also survived. *USN photo*

American dive-bombers. Dauntlesses won the battle by sinking all four enemy carriers in exchange for *Yorktown*. Never again would Imperial Japan embark upon a strategic offensive.

The Battle of Midway ended the TBD's career. Devastator air crews suffered 83 percent losses, though VT-8's land-based TBF detachment did no better, sustaining 88 percent killed.

In her after-action report, *Enterprise* enumerated the reasons for heavy Devastator losses. The list bore an eerie resemblance to *Lexington's* conclusions after Coral Sea one month earlier:

(1) Skillful maneuvering of enemy ships.
(2) Interception by enemy fighters.
(3) Lack of coordination with friendly dive-bombers.
(4) Lack of coordination with friendly fighters.
(5) Enemy antiaircraft fire.

After 4 June 1942, only about three dozen Devastators remained in the navy inventory and the type disappeared from operational training in late 1944. Attempts by qualified civilian salvagers to retrieve TBD Devastators from relatively shallow water in the 1990s have repeatedly been stymied by the navy museum bureaucracy, and therefore the Devastator remains extinct.

Chapter five

Grumman TBF Avenger

Reportedly, the Grumman TBF was named "Avenger" because it was expected to avenge the surprise attack on Pearl Harbor. Wartime press releases held that the big torpedo bomber lived up to its name at Midway—a blatant example of gilding the propaganda lily—but certainly the aircraft contributed its fair share to both the Atlantic and Pacific Fleets over the next three years.

Contracted in April 1940, the XTBF-1 was nearly as revolutionary as evolutionary for a carrier-based aircraft. Bigger and much faster than Douglas' TBD it would replace, the Grumman also was far more capable. The basic design permitted an extraordinary amount of "stretch" since the large airframe easily absorbed subsequent advancement in equipment, ordnance, and missions.

With Wright's R-2600 radial engine of 1,700 horsepower mated to a huge airfoil, the basic aircraft was capable of carrier launches with exceptional loads. In fleet service the Avenger, like other strike aircraft, soon became overladen, but still possessed exceptional range and payload. By comparison,

A late-October 1944 program was developed to train 16 all-marine air groups (MCVG) to equip four new, larger *Commencement-Bay* CVEs for the war in the Pacific. The groups were to have 18 fighters and 12 torpedo bombers in two squadrons. A VMTB-132 TBM-3E is pictured about to catapult from *Cape Glouchester* (CVE-109) off Kyushu, Japan, 8 September 1945. *USMC photo, courtesy Bob Cressman*

Grumman Aircraft Engineering Corporation noted mostly for its Navy fighters, got into the attack field with the first flight of thr XTBF-1 BuNo 2539 on 1 Aug 1941 with Bob Hall as its pilot. It was lost on 28 Nov 1941 when another test pilot prematurely bailed out after a possible explosion in the bomb bay. BuNo 2538 is easily recognized by its lack of a dorsal fin extending from the vertical stabilizer to midway to the rear turret, added to later avengers. *Grumman photo, Cortesy Grumman History Center*

the Devastator's maximum mission weight was 10,200 pounds; the TBF-1 rated 13,700 while the Eastern TBM-3E-version went off the deck at a maximum weight of nearly 18,000 pounds.

The navy ordered two prototypes, with the first flight logged in August 1941. By then, however, the need for modern torpedo planes was obvious and Grumman already had a production order for 286 before the "X job" had even flown.

The TBF program suffered a setback with the loss of the first prototype in November 1941. The second airframe was ready the next month, however, and left the ground on 20 December. By then, of course, America was engaged in a two-ocean war and the navy badly needed far more than the 99 Devastators remaining in the inventory.

Casting about for a second source of new aircraft, the Bureau of Aeronautics turned to one of the world's foremost manufacturing companies. In March 1942 the newly formed Eastern Aircraft Division of General Motors Corporation signed a contract to build Avengers as well as Wildcat fighters. A plant was constructed at Trenton, New Jersey, with Avenger deliveries commencing in November. Designated TBM-1s, the first 550 were nearly identical to TBF-1s, and the next 2,300 were TBM-1Cs. The definitive Avenger, the TBM-3, accounted for more than 4,600 aircraft in the 18 months from April 1944 to September 1945. Therefore, the

"dash threes" from GM accounted for nearly half of total Avenger production.

The TBM-3 had the "dash 20" version of the R-2600 engine, rated at 1,900 takeoff horsepower. Possessing slightly higher service ceiling than the TBF-1 but slightly less climb rate and range, the TBM-3 was comparable at some 230 knots.

Meanwhile, initial fleet deliveries were made in March 1942, as *Hornet's* VT-8 obtained the first TBF-1s at Norfolk, Virginia. Torpedo Eight air crews marveled at the new Grumman, which possessed three times the range of the Devastator and was more than 60 miles per hour faster.

However, *Hornet* was desperately needed in the Pacific and there was no time for America's newest carrier to await arrival of additional Avengers. She sailed with Devastators embarked while a six-plane detachment of Avengers eventually flew cross-country to San Diego and from there reached its final destination: Midway Atoll in June 1942. Five of the six VT-8 TBFs sent against Japanese carriers on 4 June were shot down, their crews killed in action. Pilot of the only surviving Avenger was Ens. Albert K. "Bert" Earnest, who became the first of just three Avenger pilots to receive two Navy Crosses. Earnest's niche in history was unique in that both his decorations were awarded for the same mission: one for his attack on the Japanese carriers, the other for his dogged determination in bringing his crippled Grumman back to Midway with a wounded radioman and dead gunner.

The reorganized VT-8 also produced the Avenger's second double recipient of the Navy Cross. Lt. Bruce Harwood attacked Japanese ships during two Guadalcanal actions, and earned an unprecedented third Navy Cross as a torpedo pilot in the Battle of Leyte Gulf in October 1944.

By the time of the Guadalcanal landings in August 1942, all Pacific Fleet VT units had re-equipped with TBFs. U.S. Marine Corps as well as Navy Avengers contributed to the destruction of a carrier and a battleship during the campaign, in addition to several merchant and transport vessels. Between them, the Wildcat and Avenger were what Secretary of the Navy James Forrestal had in mind when he said, "Grumman saved Guadalcanal."

With ample room for a radar set and operator, the Avenger became a leading player in the carrier night war. *Enterprise* TBFs conducted the first radar-guided nocturnal attacks in U.S. Navy history during operations

As was the TBD, the TBF was designed to carry a bombardier in the cockpit aft of the pilot. This position was normally not used by operational units. The first Avengers were equipped with a fixed .30-caliber machine gun in the starboard cowling, a .50-caliber in the rear turret, and a flexible .30-caliber in the ventricle window. TBF-1 over Long Island c. early 1941. *Grumman photo, courtesy Grumman History Center*

Initial deliveries of the TBF-1 began in May 1942 with VT-8, operating as a split unit with TBD Devastators on board *Hornet* (CV-8) along with a training and familiarization detachment at Norfolk operating Brewster SBN-1s while awaiting the Avenger. VT-8 crew poses with BuNo 00830, the first -1 delivered to the fleet. *Grumman photo, courtesy Grumman History Center*

This mid-1942 photo of an early TBF-1 Avenger demonstrates the difficulty of dating photographs by national insignia or paint schemes. Although upper right and lower left insignia were removed from the wings 26 February 1941, this aircraft still has them in all four positions. Red circles were removed from the insignia 6 May 1942. *Rudy Arnold coll., courtesy Grumman History Center*

Lightly armored with machine guns, the big torpedo bomber packed a good payload with the capability of hauling 1,600 pounds of bombs or a torpedo internally. Later, rockets were also carried under the wings. A TBF-1 is pictured here out of Bethpage, c. mid-1942. *Grumman photo, courtesy Grumman History Center*

against Truk Atoll the night of 16–17 February 1944. A dozen Avengers, each armed with four 500-pound bombs, dropped one bomb per pass, aiming at the water line of Japanese freighters anchored in the lagoon. Making 150 knots airspeed at 250 feet, Torpedo 10 scored 50 percent hits resulting in assessment of 13 ships sunk, beached, or damaged. Under cover of darkness the big

Grummans avoided most of the flak, losing one aircraft and crew.

After 1942's miserable showing with aerial torpedoes, the U.S. Navy redressed the many technical faults of the Mark 13. Some measure of the improved ordnance was provided by VT-17 aboard *Bunker Hill* (CV-17) during the same Truk raid. Torpedo 17 dropped 37

A rarely seen dorsal "stinger" .30-caliber gun is visible in the lead aircraft of the flight of TBF-1s, c. mid-1942. This gun was manned by the radioman/radar operator. *Grumman photo, courtesy Grumman History Center*

torpedoes in the big lagoon, claiming 18 hits, which sank a light cruiser on the first day and a destroyer the next; airmen reported that it sank in 90 seconds. One torpedo, dropped a bit later than the others, passed directly *over* the crumbling destroyer *Tachikaze* as she slid out of sight, resulting in a frustrating "miss" credited to the pilot. *Bunker Hill's* Avengers also sank two oilers and two cargo ships.

The "Big E" and *Independence* Avengers also pioneered full-time night air group operations, including the first electronic countermeasures missions in carrier aviation history. Comdr. William I. Martin, formerly skipper of VT-10, took Night Air Group 90 to combat in 1945 and remained aboard until *Enterprise* was knocked out of the war by a *kamikaze* pilot that May.

The "Quiet Hero," self-effacing Capt. Albert K. "Bert" Earnest, USN (Ret), was an ensign when he flew his VT-8 TBF-1 from Midway to attack the Japanese Fleet. The only TBF pilot to survive the battle, he brought his Avenger back to Midway with a dead radioman and wounded gunner. Bert Earnest earned two Navy Crosses at Midway, the first of three he received during World War II. *USN photo, courtesy Capt. A. K. Earnest, USN (Ret)*

By the Battle of Midway (4–6 June 1942), VT-8's Avengers had arrived at NAS Ford Island. Six of the bombers were hastily flown to the atoll to bolster the attack forces there. Of the six VT-8 TBF-1s that attacked the Japanese Fleet, only one returned to Sand Island. Ens. Albert K. "Bert" Earnest, brought his badly damaged BuNo 00830 back to Midway with his turret gunner, Aviation Machinist Mate 3rd class J. D. Manning, dead, and radioman, Aviation Machinist Mate 3rd class Harry D. Ferrier, wounded. BuNo 8-T-1 is at Midway following Bert Earnest's intrepid return flight with most of his controls and hydraulics shot out. *USN photo*

The second production model Avenger was the TBF-1C—it differed from the -1 by the removal of the .30-caliber gun in the cowling, and the addition of two .50-caliber guns in the wings. Later -1Cs had ASB radar installed with "Yaggi" antennas under the wings along with rocket rails. TBF-1C is at Grumman's Bethpage plant, c. mid-1942. *Grumman, courtesy Jeff Ethell*

THE U-BOAT WAR

Avengers flying from escort carriers prosecuted the ambivalent war against Axis submarines in the Atlantic and Pacific. Ambivalent because by its very nature, antisubmarine warfare (ASW) involves hundreds of dull, uneventful flight hours punctuated by rare moments of anticipation and excitement. Sub contacts were rare; rarer still was an attack; rarest of all a confirmed sinking. But Avengers had a lock on carrier-based ASW in the U.S. Navy, and they achieved results.

In the Atlantic, composite squadrons were credited with 35 submarine kills, including one Japanese boat on a liaison mission. The champion U-boat killer was VC-9, which deployed in *Bogue* (CVE-9) and *Card* (CVE-11), destroying nine enemy submarines. Other "ace" units were VC-13 in *Core* (CVE-13) and *Guadalcanal* (CVE-60)

VT-8's Avengers lived up to their name when they assisted in the sinking of the Japanese light carrier IJNS *Ryujo* 24 August 1942 while flying from *Saratoga* (CV-3). Here, a TBF-1 is given the launch signal, c. late 1942. *USN photo*

Beside serving with the then-"big deck" fleet carrier, the Avenger began assignment to the smaller CVE- and CVL-class ships in 1942. A VGS-29 TBF-1 (possibly BuNo 00564) is on *Santee's* (ACV-29) elevator in August 1942. *USN photo*

with six kills and VC-1 in *Card* and the first *Block Island* (CVE-21) with five confirmed.

Sub hunting required enormous patience. One of the most successful hunter-killers was Rear Adm. Daniel V. Gallery, who described some of the problems faced by his CVE Avenger crews flying "Turkeys." He recalled in his vivid memoir, *U-505*:

"We prowled through our assigned area with the carrier 3,000 yards behind a screen of five destroyer escorts, using our airplanes to scour the ocean 100 miles on each side of our base course and 160 miles ahead. With four 'Turkeys' you could, during a four-hour flight, cover 20,000 square miles.

"But sub hunting is dull, tedious business 99 percent of the time . . . our planes could only spot U-boats when

A flight deck director signals a TBF-1 pilot onto the port catapult. By August 1942, all Pacific Fleet torpedo squadrons, most of which had been decimated at Midway, were reformed and equipped with -1 Avengers. *USN photo*

Grumman's prowess of producing successful carrier aircraft for the navy was evident by mid-1942 when two of the three aircraft types assigned to each carrier group were built by the "Iron Works." Here, a VT-5 TBF-1 launches from *Yorktown* (CV-10) for a raid on Marcus Island 31 August 1943. This attack also initiated Grumman's F6F Hellcat into battle. *USN photo*

they were surfaced. One of the hardest ideas to sell a young 'Turkey' pilot on a four-hour night patrol is that there really are submarines in an area his pal has just finished patrolling. There can be three or four U-boats in a 20,000-square-mile area that you are patrolling constantly, and you may never see them."

Of the rare occasions when a contact was prosecuted to the finish, Gallery said, "This is a tremendously exciting game which may go on for 24 hours. Sleep is just out of the question until the game is over because the jackpot

did not involve a sinking. In June 1944, near the Azores, Gallery's *Guadalcanal* group forced *U-505* to the surface and allowed the crew to abandon ship. Believing that the scuttling charges would prevent their boat's capture, the Germans took to the water and were rescued by destroyers of Gallery's screen. Meanwhile, covered by TBMs and FM Wildcats, a prebriefed boarding party courageously entered the submarine, disarmed the charges, and emerged with code and communications intelligence of immense value. *U-505* was towed to port where she could

CV-10 had a capability unique to only five carriers, athwartship hangar deck catapult. The only combat use of this feature was when *Yorktown* (CV-10) launched strikes against Kwajalein in December 1943. CinCUS Fleet had authorized their removal 17 February 1943. A VT-5 TBF-1 launches from *Yorktown's* hangar deck May 1943. *USN photo*

Jimmy Flatley's Air Group 5 operated from *Yorktown* (CV-10) during April 1943 to May 1944, most of the time in the combat zone. A VT-5 Avenger climbs out after launch from CV-10 31 August 1943. *USN photo*

be examined for technical information, while en route VC-58 Avengers continued landing as the "tame" U-boat trailed in the CVE's wake.

There was far less opportunity for submarine stalking in the Pacific, but PacFleet CVEs proved equal to the challenge. CompRon 13 added to its Atlantic laurels with two confirmed kills while deployed in *Anzio* (CVE-57), while the same ship's VC-82 sank three Japanese submarines. Two more enemy fleet boats and an unknown number of miniature subs were hunted to destruction by CVE Avengers.

Apart from these "solo" kills, escort carrier Avengers and Wildcats also assisted destroyers of their respective task units in sinking other submarines: 19 U-boats and half a dozen Japanese I-types. But confirmed sinkings were only the visible tip of the antisubmarine iceberg. The larger success lay in the unknown and unknowable number of Axis submarines that were forced down by CVE aircraft, either thwarting or preventing an attack on Allied merchantmen and warships.

More than 20 Marine Corps squadrons flew Avengers from 1942 to 1945, including at least four assigned to escort carrier air groups (CVEGs). However, the majority of leatherneck combat TBF Avengers were land-based units in the Solomon Islands, defending Guadalcanal or participating in the reduction of the Japanese base at Rabaul, New Britain.

With an eventual average of 230 Avengers coming off the production lines every month, a surplus quickly built up. The logical outlet for the excess was the Royal Navy, which had no carrier aircraft comparable to the U.S. Navy torpedo bomber. The Avengers were renamed the Tarpon in British service (a fish of the Western Atlantic), and initial deliveries were made at NAS Quonset Point, Rhode Island, in January 1943. These were the first of some 400 TBFs and nearly 550 TBMs that served in 15 Fleet Air Arm squadrons. The Royal Navy reverted the name to Avenger in early 1944, by which time HMS *Victorious* already had introduced the type to combat in the Southwest Pacific. The Royal New Zealand Air Force also received 48 Grummans during 1943.

GENERAL MOTORS AVENGERS

With Grumman increasingly committed to the F6F Hellcat, an alternate source of torpedo planes was sought. It was quickly found in the newly formed

Eastern Aircraft Division of General Motors Corporation. Beginning in November 1942, the Eastern plant at Trenton, New Jersey, assembled TBM-1s from Grumman parts and by June 1943 was building 75 "home grown" Avengers per month. Grumman built its last TBF in December of that year, for a total of nearly 2,300 since 1941. From that point, the GM plant went from record to record, eventually peaking at 400 TBM-3 in March 1945.

From the pilot's perspective, the Avenger was an extremely "honest" aircraft with no vices. Despite its size—the largest carrier aircraft of its day—it was relatively easy to get aboard carriers owing to its stability and docile flight characteristics. Pilots inevitably complained of the sluggish control responses, especially the heavy ailerons, but agility was seldom an operational requirement for the roles of reconnaissance, bombing, or antisubmarine patrol.

Following its successful battles at Midway and Guadalcanal, the navy in 1944 began an aggressive carrier campaign against Japanese installations in the Pacific. Unidentified squadron TBF-1C are caught here over Wotje Atoll after a Marshall Islands raid 9 February 1944. *USN photo, PhoM1/c Edward M. Greenwood*

Lexington's (CV-16) Air Group 16 aircraft mix is demonstrated in this November 1943 photo showing the flight deck crew on the wing of an SBD-5 as a TBF-1 taxis forward and an F6F-3 comes aboard. *USN photo, Commander Edw. Steichen*

Both PacFlt and LantFlt Advanced Carrier Training Groups (ATCG) intensified their operations to qualify combat aircrews, often using recently commissioned CVEs, which also helped train the carrier crews. Here, an ACTG Pac TBF-1C has just landed aboard a PacFlt CVE. *USN photo*

Lt. Henry "Hank" Suerstedt was an experienced Avenger pilot who flew TBFs and TBMs against the Japanese from the escort carriers *Marcus Island* as well as *Commencement Bay*, and commanded a postwar TBM squadron. His assessment of the type addressed the challenge of landing a large aircraft on a small deck: "Aerodynamically, the TBM was an extremely predictable aircraft, though somewhat cumbersome. When coming aboard in bad weather on a pitching deck, on a few occasions when slow and high at the 'cut,' once the nose dropped through, the aircraft required a momentary burst of full power in order to get the tail down. This kept the aircraft from dropping to the deck nose-down on the main landing gear, but it was most stimulating to roll to a stop, arrested by number two or three wire, and hear the air officer's

Nine CVLs were converted from cruiser hulls under construction during World War II to add more fast carrier capability to Pacific Fleet task forces. *Monterey* (CVL-26) flight deck and Air Group 30 air crews prepare for launch in late 1943. *USN photo*

Incredibly, although longer and heavier, the *Independence*-class CVLs had only a 73-foot-wide flight deck, 7 feet narrower than the smallest CVE. A VC-25 (redesignated VT-25, 15 December 1943) TBF-1C returns from a Marshalls raid in late 1943. *USN photo*

In the Atlantic, Avengers served on board CVEs in ASW roles, combating Germany's submarine wolf packs. Lant-Flt VC squadrons were credited with 35 submarine kills, including a hapless Japanese boat on a liaison mission. A TBF-1C comes aboard *Charger* (CV-30) dressed in the Atlantic ASW paint scheme, 22 April 1944. *USN photo*

Three types of TF 58 carriers are represented in this photo of VT-16 TBF-1Cs landing on board *Lexington* (CV-16) (*Essex* class) as *Enterprise* (CV-6) (*Yorktown* class) steams in on the left side of the photo and *Princeton* (CVL-23) (*Independence* class) steams astern. *USN photo*

Avenger "Torpeckers" also served land-based throughout the Pacific War with both USN and USMC units. VT-26 TBM-3s are shown here at a Philippines airstrip, c. October 1944. With Grumman's production capacity stretched to the limit, Avenger production was contracted out to General Motors' Eastern Aircraft Division under the designation TBM. *USN photo*

Yellow markings and V-lettering identifies an Advanced Carrier Training Group Pacific TBM-3 Avenger taxiing into position on the port catapult of a PacFlt CVE. *USN photo*

Four MCVGs made it to the combat zone before hostilities ended 15 August 1945. MCVG-1 in *Block Island* (CVE-106) and MCVG-2 in *Gilbert Islands* (CVE-107), participated in the Okinawa campaign and Balikpapan invasion. MCVG-4 in *Cape Glouchester* (CVE-109) shot down four recon planes off the China coast and MCVG-3 in *Vella Gulf* (CVE-111) arrived at Okinawa as the war ended. A plane director brings a VMTB-132 TBM-3E into tension on *Cape Glouchester's* catapult, 8 September 1945. *USMC photo, courtesy Bob Cressman*

'crash yodeler' still warbling and find yourself surrounded by the crash and rescue team."

The standard crew was pilot, turret gunner, and radioman, who often doubled as radar operator. A turret view of the war was provided by Lester Ludwig, a gunner in VMTB-242 who flew strikes from Bougainville during 1944. He recalled, "The turret was equipped with a single .50-caliber machine gun, which was fed from the underside by a can holding the ammunition. The .50 was on the left side of the gunner, shoulder high. In front was a pistol grip used for control of the turret and trigger for the gun, with bulletproof glass in front of the gunner. He had to climb up into the seat and pull the armor plate up under him. He was well protected except from the top and right side of the turret. The gun controls had automatic shutoff switches so the tail or wingtip wouldn't be hit when we fired. One pilot thought they worked all the time and told his gunner to try it. The gunner shot off the wingtip!"

Though a bombardier could be carried behind the pilot, the Norden bomb sight originally installed in Avengers was almost never used in combat because early on the navy recognized the futility of trying to hit a maneuvering ship

VMTB-132 TBM-3E comes aboard CVE-109 at dusk after a patrol mission over Kyushu, 8 September 1945. Marine air groups continued to deploy in CVEs after the war and returned to combat from them in Korea. *USMC photo, courtesy Bob Cressman*

from high altitude. Far more Avenger sorties were flown with bombs than torpedoes, and the most common attack mode was a shallow dive to release four 500-pounders from about 1,500 feet.

For Pacific Fleet air crews, a typical Avenger mission averaged 3.5 hours, though more than 5 hours airborne

The Avenger continued serving with the fleet until 1954 and with reserve forces until 1956. Here, a VA-10A TBM-3E lands aboard *Philippine Sea* (CV-47) during her 1947 Med cruise. *Commander John Moore, USN (Ret)*

The Avenger's World War II success as an ASW platform was followed by its extensive use with the navy's postwar Hunter-Killer ASW groups. The TBM-3 was modified also as a "hunter" and "killer" with a search version, the TBM-3W, and the attack version, TBM-3S (and later -3S2). Below, VS-871 TBM-3W (top) and TBM-3S2s conduct ASW operations from *Bataan* (CVL-29) during January 1953. *Buzz Hopf*

Another postwar use of the versatile Avenger airframe was the TBM-3R carrier-onboard-delivery (COD) version used extensively during the Korean War. Modified from the basic TBM-3, the -3Rs had a seven-seat capacity and provisions for carrying cargo in the torpedo bay. A VR-23 TBM-3R is shown here on a COD mission off Korea in 1953. *Royce Harper photo, courtesy Mike Maule*

was possible, with nearly 9 hours during two missions in one day. Most pilots and air crewmen logged 40 to 50 hours per month in the combat zone, flying a variety of missions: bombing; antiship strikes, including torpedo attacks; close air support; searches; and antisubmarine patrol. Special mission tasks included electronic countermeasures, mine laying, and fleet exercises.

Throughout the Pacific War, Avengers hauled more than their share of the load. Between them, the carrier-based Grumman and Eastern bombers delivered 24,500 tons of bombs, or nearly twice the combined total of Dauntlesses and Helldivers. On antishipping strikes, as Avengers flew 5,700 sorties against Japanese merchant and combatant vessels, while the dive-bombers accounted for 6,500. As a share of the total, Avengers represented 47 percent of carrier-launched missions against enemy shipping. With reduction of SB2C squadrons in the fast carriers during 1945, the Avenger's importance only increased, reaching 62 percent of bomb tonnage dropped.

On the other side of the ledger, Avengers recorded the lowest loss rate per sortie for carrier aircraft: a mere 1.69 percent, compared to 2.16 for the SBD and 2.68 for the SB2C.

The TBM's illustrious operational career in the fleet ended October 1954 when VS-27 retired its last TBM-3E. Avengers continued serving with the Naval Air Reserve until the mid-1950s in VS squadrons. NARTU Denver TBM-3Es and -3S2s are caught in flight over the plains of Colorado in 1955. *Bob Lawson*

Following its wartime successes as an attack bomber and postwar multimission roles in the fleet, the Avenger assumed a valuable postwar civilian role as an airborne firefighter (air tanker). Several civilian Avengers are still flying, most of them ex-aerial tankers, one of which is Jeff Clyman's TBM-3E BuNo 85886 seen at Farmingdale, New York, 25 May 2000. *Lynn McDonald*

Avenger production accelerated dramatically during the war, from 649 TBF-1s during 1942 to more than four times as many in 1943. That year, General Motors' mass production expertise kicked into high gear with 1,109 TBMs—nearly as many as Grumman's 1,645. However, during 1944 the Eastern Aircraft Division of GM rolled out 3,481 Avengers, or slightly more than combined Grumman-GM production in the previous two years. Another 2,953 were delivered before production ended in October 1945.

In all, 9,837 Avengers were delivered from 1942 to 1945, far more than any other naval strike aircraft in history. TBMs continued in service decades after VJ-Day, serving increasingly in antisubmarine and utility squadrons. During the Korean War TBM-3Rs were employed as carrier onboard delivery aircraft (CODs) bringing passengers, spare parts, and (most important) parcels and mail to attack carriers. Avengers also evacuated casualties from the hard-pressed Marine Corps perimeter at the Chosin Reservoir that bitter, hard-fought winter of 1950.

Lexington (CV-16) pilots attend prestrike briefing in one of the *Essex*-class carrier's ready rooms, c. 1943–1944. *USN photo*

AvGas is loaded into a TBF-1 by an ACTG Pac CVE refueling crew, c. mid-1943. During World War II, refueling crews wore red jerseys; later they were switched into purple jerseys and were usually referred to as "grapes." *USN photo*

Designed specifically as a torpedo bomber, the TBF was most often used in the latter role, functioning in both horizontal and glide-bombing. "Ordie" prepares a general-purpose bomb for loading, c. mid-1942. *USN photo*

Chapter six

They Also Served

The U.S. Navy's four scout-bombers and torpedo planes that fought from carrier decks were not wholly alone. The previous generation of naval strike aircraft was represented by a variety of biplanes and monoplanes, while the follow-on models from at least four manufacturers pointed the way to the future.

VOUGHT SBU

Excepting the SBD and SB2C, no fewer than five scout-bomber types overlapped the transition period from peacetime to wartime naval service. The earliest was the Vought SBU, a conventional fixed-gear biplane with angular good looks that served its last days flying neutrality patrols in the North Atlantic. The 126 Voughts remained in the fleet from 1935 to April 1941, when Scouting 41 became Fighting 42 with F4F-3 Wildcats. Despite its small numbers, the "Sugar Baker Uncle" provided many wartime aviators with initial fleet experience that prepared them for more potent weapon platforms later on.

At the beginning of World War II, some U.S. Navy and Marine Corps units were still operating Curtiss SBC-4 biplanes. The SBC was Curtiss' original Helldiver, the first of which had entered service in 1937 with VS-5. VMO-151 SBC-4 is in flight c. early 1941, wearing the overall light gray camouflage scheme of January–August 1941. *USN photo, courtesy Jeff Ethell*

CURTISS SBC

The last carrier-based biplane in U.S. Navy service was the big Curtiss SBC, unofficially called "Helldiver" even before its monoplane successor assumed the name. First flown in 1934 and joining the fleet in 1937, the SBC was largely replaced by SB2Us and SBDs in carrier squadrons before Pearl Harbor, though *Hornet* Air Group retained them in December 1941. The marines, however, operated an SBC squadron as late as June 1943, with VMO-151 based in the backwater theater of American Samoa.

Of 258 total aircraft, 50 SBC-4s were transferred to French and British control in 1940. The British SBCs were called Clevelands but apparently were never flown operationally.

CURTISS SB3C

The Helldiver's intended successor was the SB3C-1. Like the SB2C, it featured an internal bomb/torpedo bay but added wing racks for two 500-pounders. Overtaken by events, the SB3C proved a dead-end project, with two

As World War II began in Europe, two navy carrier squadrons were still operating the obsolete Vought SBU-1 biplane. A VS-41 SBU-1 assigned to *Ranger* (CV-4) is on a 1941 Atlantic mission here, wearing neutrality patrol national insignia on its engine cowl. *Capt. Brainard Mc-Comber, courtesy John Lundstrom*

Lt. Comdr. Miles R. Browning, commander, *Yorktown* Air Group in 1938, selected the Northrop BT-1 BuNo 0633 for his personal aircraft. The aircraft was destroyed in a water crash 15 April 1943 while at NAS Miami. *Wm. F. Yeager photo*

Neither of Brewster's SBA or follow-on SB2A Buccaneer designs made it to World War II combat with U.S. forces. The SB2A was used mainly with the Naval Air Operational Training Command (NAOTC). Some SB2A-4s were used by the marines as night fighter trainers. Here, NAOTC SB2A-4 from NAAS Vero Beach, Florida, is on a training flight 20 May 1943. *USN photo*

By 7 December 1941, 100 Vought SB2U-1s were flying with USMC squadrons but would be replaced by SBDs and TBFs by mid-1942. The only combat use of the Vindicator was during the Battle of Midway, when VMSB-241, operating both SBDs and SB2Us, launched several of the latter against Japanese attacking forces. VMSB-131 SB2U-3s in flight above and below during man-up in 1941. *USN photo, courtesy Jeff Ethell*

prototypes ordered by the navy but never completed. It was one of the last designs by the ill-fated Curtiss company, which failed to survive the postwar downturn in military spending.

NORTHROP BT

Northrop's BT dive-bomber was a racy-looking monoplane that equipped bombing squadrons in *Yorktown* and *Enterprise* from 1938 to 1940. With semi-retractable landing gear and an effective set of dive flaps, the BT showed the way to the future. The last of 54 BTs disappeared from navy rosters in April 1943, but by then their successor Dauntlesses had made their mark.

Designer Edward H. Heinemann had fond memories of the BT, as he described in his memoir: "It was customary in those days for the designer to ride in the rear seat with the pilot whenever possible on test flights. This practice was valuable for technical as well as psychological reasons. It demonstrated to fellow employees that the designer had confidence in his product! Of equal importance, the designer served as a professional observer to assist the pilot. This custom endured with most multiplace airplanes until the war started. After that, it was viewed as an unnecessary risk."

The BT-1 bore a family resemblance to the follow-on Douglas SBD-1, with the XBT-2 serving as midwife to

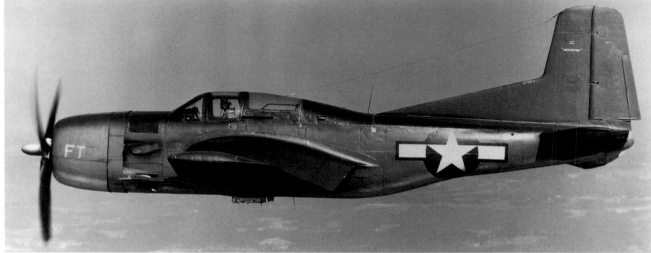

In mid-1941, the navy ordered two prototype XSB2D-1s as replacements for the SBDs just barely getting to the fleet. The new design was first flown 8 April 1943, but quickly evolved into the XBTD-1 Destroyer, which was to be a new class of single-seat torpedo bombers. Only 28 BTD-1s were delivered before cancellation of the project, and none served operationally. Top, XSB2D-1 BuNo 03351 on a 1945 Douglas test flight. *Douglas Photo, courtesy Harry Gann*

Above, the follow-on BTD-1 BuNo 04962 is on a 25 July 1944 test flight while assigned to NATC Patuxent River's Flight Test Division. *USN photo*

Another also-ran in the late-war attack design competitions was Douglas' XTB2D-1 torpedo bomber. Two prototypes of the three-place aircraft were completed before the project was cancelled in 1945. BuNo 36933 is at El Segundo, California, 26 February 1945. *Douglas photo, courtesy Ray Wagner*

the Dauntless. When Northrop's El Segundo plant was sold to Douglas, the scout-bomber project remained in-house, and Ed Heinemann's team saw the prototype "dash two" take to the air in August 1938. With a few changes—most notably to the empennage—the XBT-2 emerged as the SBD-1 in 1940, and the rest, as they say, is history.

BREWSTER SBA/SB2A

Brewster Aeronautical Company led a checkered career, with its most famous product the ill-fated F2A Buffalo fighter. However, the SBA scout-bomber enjoyed far less success than the Buffalo, and only 31 were built. Even then, however, production was undertaken by the Naval Aircraft Factory in Philadelphia owing to the parent firm's inability to manufacture its own design. First flown in 1936, the SBN was delivered to Torpedo Eight in August 1941, pending the expected availability of Avengers.

Far more numerous were 770 Brewster Model 340s: SB2A Buccaneers built for the U.S. armed forces plus Britain and the Dutch East Indies. The 162 dive-bombers intended for the DEI went to the U.S. Marine Corps after the East Indies fell to the Japanese juggernaut, while Britain's 468 Bermudas also became noncombat assets. Though fast and heavily armed, the 340 series reached maturity far too late for fleet service, and the last known examples were scrapped in the spring of 1945.

VOUGHT SB2U

The SB2U Vindicator was the second U.S. carrier-based monoplane in fleet service. Following the TBD by two months, the first SB2U-1s went to Bombing Three in December 1937, affording the navy a fairly modern scout-bomber. However, the 54 early "Wind Indicators" were seldom regarded as wholly satisfactory dive-bombers owing to their peculiar brake system: a reversible pitch propeller.

Foreign customers for the Vindicator were found in Europe. The French Navy ordered 40 V-156Fs in early 1939, with delivery that summer, just in time for the next war. In some ways the export models were superior to the U.S. Navy's aircraft, as the French insisted on armor plate and conventional dive flaps. Two *flotilles* (naval squadrons) flew the Voughts, most of which were lost in the German blitzkrieg of May 1940.

A second *Aeronavale* order of 50 SB2U-3s had been placed in March 1940, but France capitulated two months later. Consequently, the order was taken over by Britain, and the designation became V-156B, called the *Chesapeake*. Delivery began in March 1941, but as short-handed as the RAF and Fleet Air Arm were, the type was never committed to combat. Orders for 57 "dash threes" raised total production to 260 Vindicators.

The undisputed winner of the late-war new attack design between Martin's XBTM-1 and Douglas' XBT2D-1 was the latter, which in 1947 became the famed AD Skyraider, without a doubt, the world's most efficient prop-driven attack aircraft ever built. First flight was 18 March 1945 with LaVerne Brown as test pilot of the Wright R-3350-24W–powered bomber. BuNo 09085, the first of 3,180 Skyraiders and experimental XBT2D-1s built, is in flight out of El Segundo, California, 29 August 1945. *Douglas photo, courtesy Harry Gann*

Another "almost was" is Vought's TBU Seawolf design, of which only 180 were produced as TBY-2s built by Consolidated-Vultee. Although the TBY-2s served in several squadrons, mainly VT-154, and never in squadron strength, the Seawolf died a quiet death in mid-1945 after only a few months in the fleet. Here, TBY-2s of VT-154, commanded by Lt. Comdr. George Gay, VT-8's only TBD survivor at Midway, are in flight from NAS Quonset Point, Rhode Island, 10 July 1945. *USN photo, courtesy Don Bratt*

Martin's XBTM-1 Mauler was the third of four 1943–1944 single-seat attack designs, first flown by O. E. "Pat" Tibbs, 26 Aug 1944. The Mauler was in direct competition with Douglas' XBT2D-1 Dauntless II. Redesignated AM-1 in 1947, the Mauler had only limited success as a fleet aircraft and was phased out in 1950 after only two years service. Depicted here, an NATC XBTM-1 85162 during a 1945 test flight from Pax River. *USN photo*

At the time of Pearl Harbor, VMSB-131 in Hawaii had SB2U-3s, several of which were destroyed on the ground, while VMSB-232 at Quantico also flew "dash threes." Meanwhile, in the Atlantic Fleet "dash twos" equipped four scouting squadrons aboard *Ranger* (CV-4) and *Wasp* (CV-7).

Though *Wasp* took VS-71 and -72 on Atlantic deployments during 1942, the Vindicator's only combat occurred six months after Pearl Harbor. VMSB-241, land based at Midway in June 1942, counted 21 SB2U-3s in addition to 18 SBD-2s. The Vindicators sustained six losses in three missions, two of which contacted the enemy. One Vindicator pilot, Capt. Richard E. Fleming, was awarded a posthumous Medal of Honor for his attack on the Japanese battlecruiser *Mogami*.

The SB2U was last reported in service in February 1943.

FOUR FROM DOUGLAS

A late-blooming design from El Segundo was the abortive SB2D Dauntless II. First flown in April 1943, the 7-ton, crank-winged attack bomber had a 44-foot span with an interior bomb bay but failed to meet design specs (particularly weight) and was cancelled in June 1944 after 30 airframes were built. Concluded test pilot LaVerne Brown, "She's nothing to write home about."

Following the SB2D setback, Douglas attempted to revive its own project with a somewhat larger, heavier aircraft designated BTD. Eight Destroyers were produced for evaluation at the Naval Air Test Center. Some Douglas partisans felt that the evaluation program at NAS Patuxent River was conducted by pilots who favored other manufacturers, but whatever the cause, the BTD went nowhere.

An even bigger airplane was the Douglas TB2D Skypirate torpedo bomber, with two prototypes ordered in October 1943. Powered by a Pratt & Whitney R-4360 turning twin contra-rotating propellers, the Skypirate anticipated fleet introduction of the new Midway- carriers. Intended to carry four torpedoes, the TB2D weighed 9 tons empty with a 70-foot wingspan. Complexity of the hydraulic system plus propeller control difficulties delayed the project beyond reasonable hope of committing it to combat, and the program was cancelled in 1945.

Salvaging funds remaining from the Destroyer program, Ed Heinemann and his design team started from scratch. After three consecutive losses they badly needed a winner, and they got it. The result was the incredibly versatile Skyraider.

Contracted in July 1944, the Douglas BT2D Dauntless II, later renamed Skyraider, became a landmark in

The more successful Grumman design as a replacement for the Avenger was its XTB3F-1, which would evolve into the AF Guardian of the 1950s. Designed in 1944, the XTB3F-1 was to be a higher performance torpedo bomber with a conventional Pratt &Whitney R-2800-34W engine in the nose and a Westinghouse 19XB jet in the aft fuselage. BuNo 90504 "Fertile Myrtle," the first prototype, is in flight c. 1947 at Bethpage. *Grumman History Center*

Intending to replace the Avenger, Grumman designed a modified version of the F7F Tigercat as a twin-engine attack carrier plane. Design 55, designated XTSF-1, then redesignated XTB2F-1, was proposed in December 1942 but never advanced beyond a one-sided wooden mock-up seen here 11 June 1944 at Bethpage. The project was canceled in January 1945 when it became apparent the aircraft would be too big and heavy for carrier operations. *Grumman History Center, courtesy Andrè Hubbard*

tailhook aviation. Bigger and heavier than the dead-end BTD, it was the first type designed as a generic attack aircraft, combining the dive and torpedo bomber roles. Douglas, fresh out of the SBD Dauntless business, gave the project top priority, and the prototype flew in March 1945, only eight months later. Despite problems with the Wright R-3350 engine, the Skyraider demonstrated immense potential and, as the AD, went to VA-19A in December 1946. More than 3,100 were produced through 1957, and the Skyraider served carrier aviation's medium attack role during the Korean War and, as the A-1, logged thousands of sorties with the U.S. Navy plus the U.S. and South Vietnamese Air Force in Vietnam.

VOUGHT TBU/CONSOLIDATED TBY

Vought Aircraft in Connecticut had its hands full throughout the war, producing the superb F4U Corsair fighter. However, dating from 1940 the TBU (later christened Seawolf) occupied engineering hours and plant space the company could ill afford. Therefore, after flying the XTBU-1 prototype on 22 December 1941, Vought transferred the production contract to Consolidated. The TBY-2 demonstrated decent performance behind the well-proven Pratt & Whitney R-2800 and joined VT-97 in April 1945. The need for an alternate torpedo plane disappeared before VJ-Day, however, with only 181 aircraft delivered. Vought's main contribution to the war effort remained the F4U, while Consolidated produced the beloved PBY Catalina and the B-24/PB4Y Liberator series.

MARTIN BTM/AM

The Martin BTM Mauler, contracted in January 1944, was first flown that August. Despite the airframe's rapid development, the BTM Mauler suffered perennial teething problems with the Pratt & Whitney R-4360, rated at an exceptional 3,300 horsepower. Delivered to VA-17A in 1948 (redesignated AM-1, or "Able Mable"), the Mauler's fleet life lasted only two and a half years, with the final AM-1Q versions carried by VC-4 in fall 1950. Total production was 152 aircraft, all "dash one" variants. "Able Mable" left very few aviators with lingering affection, but certainly the company more than compensated with its long-lived PBM Mariner flying boat and the tough, speedy B-26 Marauder of the Army Air Force.

GRUMMAN TB3F/AF

Grumman was never a firm to rest on its laurels, even in wartime. Consequently, a successor to the highly successful Avenger originated in February 1945 when the "Iron Works" contracted for the TB3F Guardian. Even larger than the TBF, the Guardian became a dedicated antisubmarine aircraft with variants devoted to the "hunter" and "killer" roles. The new design flew in December 1946 but did not join a fleet squadron until 1950, designated AF-1 and AF-2. The 389 AFs served in fleet units for five years, at which time they were replaced by Grummans' more versatile twin-engine S2F/S-2 Tracker.

Chapter seven

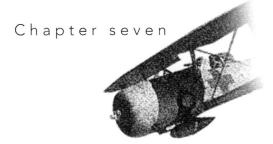

The Attack War

On the morning of 7 December 1941, USS *Enterprise* was returning from a ferry mission, delivering Marine Corps fighters to Wake Island. As a precaution, "The Big E" launched 18 SBDs of VS- and VB-6 250 miles west of Pearl Harbor, Hawaii, to scout ahead of Task Force eight. Acknowledging America's deteriorating diplomatic conditions with Japan, Vice Adm. William F. Halsey had placed his unit on a wartime footing five weeks previously.

Less than two hours later, most of the Dauntless aircrews were fighting for their lives. In the appalling confusion over Oahu, where 383 Japanese carrier planes attacked U.S. military facilities with near impunity, naval aviation sustained its first casualties in the Pacific War.

When the results were tallied that afternoon, five SBDs had been shot down by Japanese aircraft and another by American gunners. Eight *Enterprise* pilots or air crewmen were dead and three injured. Ten Dauntlesses were available at Ford Island where Lt. Comdr. Halstead Hopping organized a hurried search to the north. They

An SBD gunner checks his .30-caliber weapon on board a *Sangamon*-class escort carrier en route to Operation Torch, the November 1942 invasion of North Africa. Other flight crew members observe. *USN photo*

The combat air crewmen of World War II were full partners with their pilots in every dual-seat carrier aircraft. Enlisted air crew held aviation ratings as diversified as radioman, ordnanceman, machinist mate, electronicsman, and photographer's mate. SB2C flight crew members pose on their Helldiver, c. 1944. *USN photo*

Lt. (jg) Ronald A. Featherstone, Jr., and his radioman/gunner examine the pilots' navigation board prior to launch, c. 1945. The carrier is believed to be *Yorktown* (CV-10). *USN photo*

scouted for three hours without result, as the Japanese carriers had steamed to the northwest. Later that evening, SBDs and TBDs aboard *Enterprise* logged the first combined mission of the war, with Dauntlesses planning a set-piece attack by laying a smoke screen for the Devastators. As one senior aviator recalled, "Fortunately, we didn't find the Japanese fleet!"

Over the next 45 months, three-quarters of the men who flew into Pearl Harbor that morning would be killed, wounded, or captured. It was only the beginning of a long, hard-fought war that took U.S. carrier aviation from tragedy to eventual triumph. The combat burden was frequently placed upon junior aviators, who provided the knowledge and leadership essential for combat success. A few of the scout-bomber and torpedo plane pilots became known to the public, but hundreds did not.

Medals and decorations are a poor measure of military achievement, as no system is wholly fair or accurate. For instance, twelve navy or marine fighter pilots received Medals of Honor during World War II, but only three attack aviators were awarded the nation's highest decoration—all in 1942. Among the select few who were presented two Navy Crosses during the war, however, it was another matter. Of the 29 navy and 2 marine pilots so honored, 15 flew SBDs and 3 flew TBFs or TBMs. Nearly all were decorated for combat during the year following Pearl Harbor, when only a few hundred carrier aviators were repeatedly committed to major actions time after time. But they were not alone in their heroism—far from it. In every carrier bomber or patrol plane were enlisted air crewmen essential to completion of the mission.

COMBAT AIRCREW

The combat air crewmen of World War II were full partners in every type of naval aircraft except, of course, single-seat fighters. Whether they held ordnance or radio ratings, air crewmen were cross-trained in both disciplines, since their combat role required equal facility with gunnery and communications. They rode facing backwards in torpedo planes and dive-bombers; they manned power turrets in patrol bombers and hunkered down in the bellies of several aircraft types, focusing on radio sets or radar scopes. The air war could not have been effectively waged without them.

Far too frequently, however, the air crewmen were taken for granted or ignored altogether. A 1943 naval aviation annual contained an essay on scout-bombers, written by a senior aviator who devoted just four sentences to "the rear-seat occupant." The same volume's section on torpedo planes contained no mention of radiomen or gunners at all.

Whatever the failings of the naval bureaucracy, there were individual officers who fully appreciated "the guys in the cheap seats." Those officers were "the guys in front," the pilots of scout-bombers, torpedo planes, and patrol bombers. No better example exists than the fact that the Enlisted Aircrew Hall of Honor was instigated by retired Rear Adm. James D. Ramage, an *Enterprise* SBD squadron commander in 1944. Ramage dedicated the shrine aboard USS *Yorktown* (CV-10), "The Arlington Cemetery of Carrier Aviation," in Charleston, South Carolina, in 1997.

Regardless of their aircraft type or mission, naval bomber pilots were unanimous in their praise of combat air crewmen. Typical was the response of Lt. Comdr. Robert E. Dixon, who said of his Scouting Squadron Two air crews after Coral Sea, "The performance of all personnel of this squadron was all that could be desired. The example set by the rear-seat gunners . . . was particularly outstanding. Time and again their accurate, tenacious fire saved pilots and planes of this squadron, and made the Japs lukewarm regarding that most important item in aerial gunnery—range. As regards personnel,

Carrier torpedo and dive-bombers wreaked havoc on the Japanese throughout the Pacific War island campaign. Airfield and support facilities burn furiously following 5–6 Oct 1943 raids on Wake Island by Task Force 50. *USN Photo, Lt. Charles Kerlee*

Fast Carrier Task Force strikes against the Japanese homeland began 16 February 1945 when TF-58 aircraft hit industrial and military targets on Honshu. Carrier strikes continued until the cessation of hostilities 15 August. CVL IJNS *Amagi* lies capsized at Kure Navy Yard after it was sunk by U.S. carrier planes. *USAF photo*

Maintenance crews work on VB-5 SBD-3s on board *Yorktown* (CV-10). Bombing 5 had done its duty well during the Battle of Midway in June 1942, flying from the old *Yorktown* (CV-5), which was the navy's only carrier loss during that engagement. The Japanese Fleet lost four carriers and several other ships of the line from damage sustained mainly by navy and marine SBDs. *USN photo*

nothing more could be asked for the successful prosecution of this war."

A later testimonial came from Comdr. William S. Emerson, who flew SBDs and SB2Cs in Bombing Squadron 19:

"As far as I am concerned, our rear-seat gunners were the bravest and the best. Can you imagine riding backwards during a vertical 10,000- to 12,000-foot dive? We lost seven of these young men along with 13 pilots, both from combat and operational causes, between August 1943 and November 1944."

Those sentiments were shared by Lt. Henry A. Suerstedt, a TBF pilot who retired as a rear admiral. "Our air crewmen were, as a whole, outstanding. No doubt in World War II there was a small percentage who should have been doing something else, but the air crew did all they were trained to do, and a lot more. The radioman who flew with me in VC-21 was even checked out in the remote control system originally intended as part of the Norden bomb sight. He had only lateral control through the Pilot Position Indicator, but we practiced to the point where we could engage it as we came off the target, after regaining level flight, and the radioman could find his way more or less back to the task group."

STEPS WEST

The first tentative steps westward on the road to Tokyo were made in February and March 1942. The Pacific Fleet carriers conducted a series of hit-and-run raids against Japanese-held islands, including simultaneous strikes in the Gilberts and Marshalls on Sunday, 1 February.

Before dawn, *Enterprise* Air Group launched 46 SBDs and TBDs to bomb Roi and Kwajalein Atolls. Five Dauntlesses were lost, including the VS-6 CO, Lieutenant Commander Hopping, for minor damage to facilities. Nine more VT-6 Devastators launched the U.S. Navy's first torpedo attack, contributing to the damage of eight ships.

Meanwhile, Rear Adm. Frank Jack Fletcher's *Yorktown* group sought targets in the Gilberts. Again, the raiders inflicted minor damage for heavy loss: Eight aircraft failed to return, though most probably ditched out of fuel.

Enterprise was back in action on 24 February, striking Japan's newly conquered Wake Island. Dauntlesses attacked the airfield but the scouts lost a plane to AA fire. A subsequent raid on Marcus Island on 4 March was notable

A VB-11 SBD-3 is pushed into position by its flight deck crew on board a West Coast CVE during late 1942 workups for the squadron's combat deployment. Scheduled for assignment to *Hornet* (CV-8), VB-11 instead first flew from Henderson Field on Guadalcanal after the loss of *Hornet* at Santa Cruz in October 1942. *USN photo*

mainly for its nocturnal aspect. Arriving early over the target, the SBDs bombed by flare and moonlight, but low clouds inhibited observation. Buildings and runways were attacked, with a Dauntless lost to flak. Two years would pass before dedicated night-strike missions were flown.

America's first two-carrier operation of the war occurred on 10 March when *Lexington* and *Yorktown* struck Lae and Salamaua, New Guinea. The carriers launched 104 aircraft that overflew the Papua Peninsula, penetrating a 13,000-foot mountain range. In spite of poor torpedo performance, TBDs helped SBDs sink three ships and damaged others in exchange for one Dauntless.

In retrospect, the results achieved by these early operations probably were not worth the cost in lives and aircraft. The raids achieved two purposes, however: They provided badly needed combat experience and they exerted pressure on a powerful, all-conquering enemy by demonstrating American resolve.

CORAL SEA AND MIDWAY

With the Pacific Fleet deprived of its battleships, only two methods of continuing the war were available to Adm. Chester Nimitz: aircraft carriers and submarines. The U.S. Navy's appalling torpedo scandal deprived the latter of an effective weapon until 1943. Consequently, Nimitz was forced to rely upon his aviators.

Lt. (jg) William La Liberte flew with Lieutenant Comm-mander Upson in early stages of VT-5's and CV-10's combat career. *USN photo, Lt. Charles Kerlee*

They rewarded trust with triumph.

Meanwhile, the Imperial Japanese Navy continued its awesome string of uninterrupted victories after Pearl Harbor. The Dutch East Indies and the Philippines fell under the broadening cloak of the Greater East Asia Co-Prosperity Sphere, as Tokyo's warships swept hundreds of thousands of square miles of Allied naval presence.

Expanding southward, Japanese forces set their sights on Port Morseby, New Guinea. From that base, they could threaten Northern Australia and control the major sea lanes connecting Hawaii with British Commonwealth interests throughout the Pacific.

American code breakers deciphered the Japanese plan and gave Nimitz the critical information he needed. With enemy forces and schedules in hand, he dispatched his two available carriers to intercept the Japanese in the Coral Sea. The timing prevented *Enterprise* and *Hornet* from participating, as they were returning from the Doolittle Raid.

Lexington and *Yorktown*, operating independently, embarked a total of 71 SBDs and 25 TBDs to blunt the Japanese thrust. They were opposed by 36 Aichi dive-bombers and 39 Nakajima torpedo planes in the Carrier Striking Force built around *Shokaku* and *Zuikaku*. Additionally, light carrier *Shoho*, with 18 aircraft, escorted the enemy invasion transports bound for Morseby. The Japanese deficit in strike aircraft was largely offset by the U.S. need to devote half the Dauntlesses to scouting while Imperial Navy float-planes conducted most of the reconnaissance.

Coral Sea preliminaries opened on 4 May when Rear Adm. Frank Jack Fletcher's *Yorktown* launched two strikes against the anchorage at Tulagi, north of the main Solomons isle of Guadalcanal. Against light aerial opposition, the *Yorktowners* torpedoed a transport but 40 SBD sorties went unrewarded, partly owing to fogged-up sights in the moist tropic air.

Though Japanese carrier aircraft had sunk HMS *Hermes* off Ceylon in April, her squadron had been ashore. Consequently, the world's first true aircraft carrier duel occurred in the Coral Sea beginning the morning of 7 May. By then *Yorktown* had joined Rear Adm. Aubrey Fitch's *Lexington* unit in a rare two-carrier operation.

American reconnaissance planes found IJN *Shoho*, which provided air cover for the Port Morseby occupation force, and the U.S. task force jumped on the opportunity. Between them, *Lexington* and *Yorktown* launched 53 SBDs and 22 TBDs with "Lady Lex's" fliers first over the target. They initiated a set-piece attack according to prewar doctrine and smothered the Japanese combat air patrol. With scout-bombers diving first, a rain of 500- and 1,000-pound bombs cascaded onto the 11,000-ton carrier, covering the Devastators' ponderous approach. Though AA fire was fairly heavy from four escorting cruisers, it failed to deflect Torpedo Two, nor did the airborne Mitsubishi fighters, which were met by escorting Wildcats.

Shoho took several bombs and torpedoes, slowing as she took on water and began losing power. A quarter hour later the *Yorktowners* piled in with more bombs and torpedoes. VT-5 claimed a perfect 10 for 10 with its Mark XIII "fish," and though the Devastators' combined results were less, the effect was sufficient.

At the helm of Scouting Five was Lt. Comdr. William O. Burch, who recalled:

"One of our scouts reported that he had sighted two cruisers and two destroyers. We launched the air group. An army plane nearby picked up another force, which did have a carrier in it. While we were on the way out, I got his last word from the *Yorktown*, stating that about 50 miles from our first position we would find a carrier. I think we would have seen it anyway. It was almost on our track to the other force.

"The *Lexington* group made their dive-bomb attack just ahead of me. I watched them attack. The Jap carrier was maneuvering heavily, and I saw only one hit. The carrier then turned into the wind to launch her planes. I immediately called Joe Taylor, who had our torpedo planes, and told him we were going in. He asked me to wait because it would be at least five minutes before he could arrive on the scene. I told him I wasn't going to wait because the carrier was launching planes and I wasn't going to let them get off. I got a hit and I don't think any of the squadrons behind me missed. We really laid the bombs in that day.

"It took five minutes from the time I pushed over until the carrier was out of sight below the surface—she just ploughed herself under. She had about seven planes in the air and was launching the rest of her fighters. It seemed best to stop that."

Shoho's loss forced the Port Morseby convoy to postpone the operation until the Americans could be brought to decisive battle. That evening, while the Japanese rethought their options and tried an abortive dusk attack, American aviators relished the knowledge that they had sunk the first large enemy combatant of the war while losing only two SBDs.

The next day's combat brought less cause for celebration. By the morning of the 8th, the Japanese Navy's Fifth Carrier Division was on hand—*Shokaku* and *Zuikaku*, which had launched against Pearl Harbor five months before. Weather favored the Japanese as Vice Adm. Takeo Takagi's force steamed beneath cloudy skies while Fletcher and Fitch's units were largely in the open.

Knowing of the danger of enemy air attack, the two U.S. task groups retained substantial fighter and scout-bomber strength. Consequently, the combined weight of the strike against Takagi was 75 planes, including 39 Dauntlesses and 21 Devastators. Low ceilings and communications problems prevented a coordinated attack, and those squadrons that did find the enemy carriers faced aroused defenses, including 16 Zeroes.

Yorktown's Bombing Five executed a successful attack that damaged *Shokaku*, but at a price. Lt. Joseph Powers had stated his intention to "lay it on their flight deck," and was as good as his word. He hit the big carrier with his half-ton bomb, but his riddled Dauntless went into the water nearby while another VB-5 plane also was shot down. Torpedo Five attacked without confirmed hits, but as the *Yorktowners* pulled away, *Shokaku* was afire from two bomb hits, clearly out of the battle.

Lexington's strike was next on the scene, led by Comdr. William B. Ault. Contrary to the situation during the previous day's combat, the U.S. aerial torpedoes were completely ineffective despite courageous attacks by both TorpRons through flak and fighters. Ault took his CAG section down on *Shokaku*, but he was lost with two of his three wingmen, having claimed at least one hit. *Zuikaku* escaped damage, but her air group had already joined her sister ship's squadrons in a well-executed attack against their tormenters.

Shortly after 1100, 69 Japanese planes approached the U.S. carriers to the south of Takagi's force. They included 33 Aichi D3A dive-bombers and 18 torpedo-packing Nakajima B5Ns, escorted by 18 Zeroes. They were opposed by elements of VF-2 and -42, plus 23 SBDs deployed per doctrine on low-level torpedo plane patrol. The American assumption was that Japanese torpedo planes were similar to the TBD, but in fact the B5N (also called Type 97) was capable of nearly 200 miles per hour. The Dauntlesses of Bombing and Scouting Two plus VS-5 were caught at a serious disadvantage, largely unable to engage the Nakajimas (later called Kates) but set upon by aggressive Zeroes.

In the wave-top shootout, six SBDs were destroyed and two more were jettisoned as irreparable after landing aboard *Lexington*. Five pilots and six gunners were lost, but they had given a good account of themselves. Despite the technical and tactical disadvantages, they shot down

Lt. Comdr. Richard Upson, commanding officer of VT-5, led his TBF squadron from *Yorktown* (CV-10) during the early offensive campaign in the Pacific of late 1943. *USN photo, Lt. Charles Kerlee*

Lt. Comdr. William I. "Bill" Martin, center, was a pioneer of night attack carrier aviation. Grounded with a broken arm, Martin's VT-10 made the first radar-directed night bombing raid against Japanese shipping in Truk Atoll in February 1944. The low-level attack resulted in sinking or damaging a dozen merchantmen in exchange for the loss of one TBF and its crew. *USN photo, courtesy Vice Adm. W. I. Martin, USN (Ret)*

at least six raiders and possibly a dozen. However, *Yorktown* was damaged and *Lexington* succumbed to torpedo damage that ignited gasoline and sent her to the bottom. The American force withdrew from the Coral Sea, having prevented the occupation of Port Morseby. For the moment, at least, Northern Australia was safe.

Among the Dauntless pilots, three received particular acclaim. *Yorktown's* Lt. Powers was awarded a posthumous Medal of Honor while VS-2's Lt. (jg) William E. Hall survived serious wounds to receive a "Congressional" for his defense of *Lexington*. His squadron-mate, Ens. John Leppla with his gunner John Liska, were credited with seven shootdowns in the battle. The torpedo crews, who ran even greater risks in their slow Devastators, garnered far less notoriety but were grateful to survive Japanese flak and fighters.

Next time, the TorpRons would not be so lucky.

MIDWAY

After Coral Sea, fleet squadrons recognized the increasing vulnerability of TBDs to Japanese fighters. Consequently, most Devastators were "upgunned" from the original single .30-caliber weapon to twin mounts intended for SBD-3s. TorpRons Six and Eight of *Enterprise* and *Hornet*, respectively, received the extra weapons, but VT-3 went to war with the single swivel mount.

The Japanese Navy's most ambitious operation following Pearl Harbor occurred six months later, back in Hawaiian waters. Four fleet carriers supported by massive surface forces were assigned to escort an invasion convoy aimed at Midway Atoll. Situated 1,100 miles northwest of Oahu, Midway in Japanese hands would pose a threat to Pearl itself. Whether Japan could have sustained a naval-air complex 2,500 miles from Tokyo is uncertain; what was beyond doubt was America's need to retain Midway.

It was no easy task. With no operational battleships, Pacific Fleet commander Adm. Chester Nimitz was forced into a carrier engagement along the lines of Coral Sea. He committed his only flight decks to the battle— *Yorktown, Enterprise,* and the new *Hornet*—while cramming Midway's two islands with every available U.S. Army, Navy, and Marine Corps plane.

At sea, *Enterprise* and *Hornet* operated as one task force while *Yorktown*, hastily repaired, sailed alone. Among them the three carriers embarked six scout-bomber squadrons with SBD-2s and -3s, plus three squadrons of TBD-1s. With her Coral Sea losses made good by previously beached *Saratoga* squadrons, *Yorktown* remained a potent organization. *Enterprise* Air Group had a good deal of corporate experience while *Hornet* Air Group was, in the words of one officer, "green as grass."

Ashore, Midway's strike force comprised 16 SBD-2s and 11 SB2U-3s of VMSB-241, six brand-new TBF-1s of the VT-8 detachment, plus four Army Air Force B-26s and 19 B-17Es and three dozen PBY-5 and -5A Catalina patrol planes.

Among the carrier air groups were 109 Dauntlesses and 44 Devastators compared to Vice Admiral Nagumo's 74 Aichi D3A dive-bombers and 81 Nakajima B5N torpedo planes, plus two prototype scouts. Fighter strength amounted to 73 A6M2 Zeroes versus 81 F4F-4s. Thus, American Adms. Raymond Spruance (*Enterprise* and *Hornet*) and Frank Jack Fletcher (*Yorktown*) faced near parity of some 230 carrier aircraft, though on paper Midway's planes more than evened the odds. As events developed, the land-based aircraft exerted little direct influence upon the course of the battle. Despite post-battle AAF claims, the Flying Fortresses were wholly ineffective against maneuvering warships; the Marine Corps scout-bomber crews were ill-trained for any but shallow-angle glide bombing; and the Avengers and Marauders were too few to succeed as torpedo planes. The long-legged Catalinas scored a torpedo hit on one Japanese ship but their greatest contribution was reconnaissance and—ultimately—air-sea rescue.

The battle was joined in earnest shortly after dawn on 4 June as Midway radar detected 107 Japanese aircraft inbound from the northwest. While 25 Buffalos and Wildcats scrambled to intercept, the hodge-podge of army, navy, and marine bombers took off as well, provided with the enemy carriers' location by PBY reports. The main segment of the land-based strike was 27 SBDs and SB2Us under Maj. Lofton R. Henderson, plus VT-8's half-dozen TBFs and 4 AAF B-26 torpedo planes.

For almost 90 minutes Midway's Air Force threw itself against the flak and fighters of Nagumo's Carrier Striking Force. Arriving piecemeal, without an integrated plan, the Americans were destroyed in detail: 12 of the 27 marines; 5 of the 6 Avengers; 2 of the 4 Marauders. Fourteen Flying Fortresses also found the quarry, but were unable to coordinate with the naval aircraft. Japanese carriers and battleships escaped with barely a scratch to their gray-painted hulls.

The length and ferocity of the U.S. attack, however, threw Nagumo off balance. Events were compounded when the three carrier-based TBD squadrons arrived in succession. Largely devoid of fighter escorts, 41 Devastators attacked; four returned to their ship.

One of the most compelling accounts from Midway was written by Lt. Robert Laub of Torpedo Six, led by Lt. Comdr. Eugene Lindsey. Laub vividly described the *Enterprise* squadron's fateful attack on the Japanese Fleet:

> There wasn't time for a coordinated attack. Commander Lindsey took us in and we just picked a carrier and headed for it. There were three of them and my section headed for one of the bigger ones (the 36,000-ton *Kaga*). Almost as soon as the run started, it was every man for himself. All I can remember is concentrating on the carrier and the flak. Fighters came down on us, but I don't remember seeing them. I only heard my gunner firing.

> Torpedo Six had twin .30-caliber rear guns. We had requisitioned them from the SBD stores to beef up our rear defenses, and prior to Midway we'd put in some homemade boilerplate armor for protection. The twin .30s must have done the job, because my gunner (Radioman First Class W. C. Humphrey, Jr.) kept the fighters off us.

> We flew for five minutes through solid bursting metal. I don't know how or why, but we took very little damage. It seemed to take forever to close. The protective screen was enormous and as it moved, the carrier turned and twisted. There was no way I was going to get a bow shot. I was lucky to get any shot at all. I didn't see any other planes flying or going down. All I saw was flak and the turning carrier.

> A few miles from the carrier I was close enough to see a deck load of aircraft, their engines running up, when I released. I broke away, staying low and turned back the way I had come. I saw no other TBDs.

> It took about an hour and one-half to get back. We had four or five holes in us. Three others from *Enterprise* also made it back, but one was such a wreck that it was pushed over the side. In the space of a little over four hours, I had become the senior surviving officer of Torpedo Six.

With his Midway strike orbiting the task force, short on fuel, Nagumo belatedly learned of the presence of at least one American carrier. Further delay ensued as the second strike group was re-armed for antiship attack. Finally ready to launch against the U.S. carriers, the lead aircraft began their takeoff rolls as lookouts screamed a warning: dive-bombers overhead.

Almost from the beginning, American hopes rested with the dive-bombers. Between them, the two U.S. task forces launched 85 Dauntlesses that morning, armed with quarter- and half-ton bombs and the approximate location of *Kido Butai*. However, *Hornet*'s ineffectual air group commander took his 35 scout-bombers out of contention with a pointless 225-mile trek westward, then reversed course. Some of his SBDs diverted to Midway to refuel while all 10 F4F escorts ditched; two pilots were lost. Meanwhile, *Hornet*'s 15 TBDs tracked Nagumo to the southwest, where the independent-minded Comdr. John Waldron heroically led VT-8 to destruction, alone and unsupported.

Fortunately for the Pacific Fleet, the *Enterprise* and *Yorktown* Air Groups were far better led than the inexperienced *Hornet*'s. In a miraculous event that could only be

Some of the leading architects of the navy's carrier war in the Pacific. Clockwise from upper left: Vice Adm. John S. Mc-Cain, CTF 38; Rear Adm. Arthur W. Radford, CTG 11.2; Adm. William F. Halsey CTF 8, 16, 30, and commander 3rd Fleet; Rear Adm. Gerald F. Bogan, CTG 38.2; and Vice Adm. Marc Mitscher, CTF 38 and 58. *USN photos*

attributed to incredible luck or divine intervention, 47 SBDs arrived simultaneously overhead *Kido Butai*. Lt. Comdr. Wade McClusky's two *Enterprise* squadrons had found Nagumo at the end of a lengthy box search and wasted no time attacking. They destroyed *Akagi* and *Kaga*. Simultaneously, Lt. Comdr. Max Leslie's VB-3 from *Yorktown* rolled in on *Soryu* and got away clean, leaving her a floating oven.

The Big E's scout-bombers weren't so lucky: Nearly half were shot down or ditched out of fuel. Furthermore, the fourth enemy carrier, *Hiryu*, had quickly launched a retaliatory strike that crippled *Yorktown*. Her SBDs recovered aboard *Enterprise*, where an impromptu tactical organization was quickly scraped together. That afternoon 24 Dauntlesses led by VS-6 skipper Lt. Earl Gallaher found *Hiryu* and put her on the bottom. Nobody knew it at that moment, but the Battle of Midway had been won.

Midway aircraft pressed the retreating Japanese on the afternoon of 5 June. Six SBDs and six SB2Us executed a glide bombing attack on *Mikuma*, the Vindicators led by Capt. Richard E. Fleming. Struck by antiaircraft fire during the glide, Fleming's SB2U continued its attack, dropped at 500 feet, and reportedly smashed into the cruiser's "X" turret. Fleming and his gunner, Pfc. George Toms, both perished, though no bomb hits were confirmed.

Under the assumption that Fleming had intentionally dived into the enemy ship, he received a posthumous Medal of Honor, only the third awarded to scout-bomber pilots, and it remained the last. Over the next two years two patrol plane pilots also received their nation's highest decoration, one posthumously; no torpedo plane pilots were so honored. Compared to the 10 marine and two navy fighter pilots awarded the "Congressional" from 1941 to 1945, clearly the VSB, VT, and VP crews were under-represented.

The battle finally ended when *Yorktown* succumbed to torpedo damage on the morning of the 7th. The course of the Pacific War was irrevocably altered.

Despite an overwhelming victory, the U.S. Navy's greatest disappointment in the crucial battle was *Hornet*. Her captain, Rear Adm. Selectee Marc Mitscher, was among the service's most experienced and respected airmen, with solid achievement in the cockpit and the Bureau of Aeronautics. He went on to great things as

commander of Task Force 58's fast carriers in 1944–1945, but neither *Hornet* nor her air group were remotely ready for Midway, with weak leadership in too many senior aviator positions. The exception, of course, was Comdr. John Waldron at the helm of Torpedo Eight. As the most competent and aggressive of *Hornet's* squadron leaders, he by rights should have been air group commander but Mitscher's former BuAer crony, Comdr. Stanhope Ring, retained that position to the detriment of the American cause. Alone among the U.S. Army, Navy, and Marine Corps units committed to the battle, Ring's two squadrons of SBDs failed to find the Japanese carriers on 4 June. Waldron, however, set a course almost directly for the target and died as he lived—at the head of his TBDs. So did Lt. Comdr. Lance Massey of VT-3 and Eugene Lindsey of VT-6.

Aside from human failings, the U.S. Navy's most significant loss at Midway was the TBD Devastator torpedo plane. Only 130 had been built in 1937–1938, and by the end of May 1942 barely 80 remained. Midway put an end to the Devastator's career, which had been characterized by exceptional good fortune with no in-flight losses to enemy action. That lucky streak ran out on the morning of 4 June 1942, but fortunately Grumman's excellent TBF was by then taking up the slack.

After Midway, numerous proposals were made by fleet aviators seeking to improve operational capabilities. There was much support for airborne radar in scout-bombers, as *Enterprise* pilots opined that, had SBDs possessed search radar, *Hiryu* would have been found soon enough to save *Yorktown*.

Fighting Three's skipper, "Jimmy" Thach, had escorted VT-3 at Midway and felt strongly about future employment of torpedo planes. While acknowledging that torpedoes were an effective method of sinking ships, he felt they should only be used on targets of opportunity: to finish off ships already slowed or otherwise damaged by dive-bombers.

Senior officers disagreed, including Admiral Nimitz, who noted ruefully that Japanese aerial torpedoes worked just fine. The main problem, of course, was the poor performance of the TBD, but that had proved a self-correcting problem. With the arrival of the TBF, and eventual improvement of the Mark 13 torpedo, the navy regained a potent weapon.

VADM Marc Mitscher, Commander Task Force 38, believed his naval career to be over after the dismal performance of Hornet's air group at Midway when he was CO of the carrier. He went on however, to become one of the leading carrier task force commanders of the war. *USN photo*

GUADALCANAL AND THE SOLOMONS

Exactly eight months after the Pearl Harbor surprise, America took the offensive in World War II. On 7 August 1942, three carriers supported the marine landings in the Solomon Islands. *Enterprise, Saratoga,* and *Wasp* aircraft immediately gained control of the air over Guadalcanal and Tulagi, but Japanese response was swift and forceful. Mitsubishi G4Ms from Rabaul, New Britain, arrived with Zero escorts that same day and inflicted heavy losses on the American air groups. Concerned with preserving his precious flight decks, Vice Admiral Fletcher withdrew beyond range of Rabaul, forcing the marines' supply ships to retreat before they had fully offloaded their cargoes. The First Marine Division was thrown upon its own meager resources at "Cactus," as Guadalcanal was known for its code name.

The importance of land-based air power was obvious, however, and two weeks later the first installment of the "Cactus Air Force" touched down at Henderson Field, named for the marine squadron commander killed at Midway. A dozen SBDs of Lt. Col. Richard Mangrum's VMSB-232 arrived on 20 August, as did nearly 20 Wildcats of VMF-223. A marine rifleman, accustomed to seeing only Japanese aircraft thus far, told a correspondent, "I always thought the most beautiful sight I'd ever see would be the Golden Gate, but damned if those SBDs ain't just about the prettiest sight any man could ever wish to see."

Four days later the third carrier battle of the war was fought in adjoining waters.

Japan's continuing efforts to reinforce its Guadalcanal garrison required naval support, both surface and air. The light carrier *Ryujo* launched a strike against Henderson Field while *Enterprise* and *Saratoga* squadrons found widely dispersed enemy naval units. Comdr. Don Felt's VB- and VS-3, plus the reorganized VT-8, tackled the *Ryujo* group and left the small flattop sinking from bomb and torpedo hits. Meanwhile, the Big E's mixed scout-bomber formation under Lt. Comdr. Turner Caldwell ran out of daylight and landed ashore, where it found a warm welcome from Mangrum and the "mud marines." Enterprise Flight 300 thus became an early member of the Cactus Air Force.

Over the next few months a grinding routine evolved: Japanese ships transited the long, open stretch of water called "The Slot" trying to arrive off Guadalcanal under darkness. Henderson Field's growing brood of U.S. Navy and Marine Corps SBDs and TBFs made daylight operations risky for the Japanese, though Wildcats and U.S. Army Airacobras were occupied defending against Rabaul's seemingly endless supply of Mitsubishi bombers. A seesaw battle of attrition continued into October, as more marine and carrier squadrons were committed to the defense of Cactus. The war at sea took its own toll, as Japanese submarines again damaged *Saratoga* in late August and sank *Wasp* the following month. Units from both ships went ashore, replacing the perpetual losses to enemy action and equatorial weather.

CARRIER CLASH: ROUND FOUR

On 26 October the Japanese Army and Navy again tried to coordinate a major reinforcement of Guadalcanal, resulting in the Battle of Santa Cruz. *Enterprise* and

Hornet, again teamed together, fought four enemy flattops in a wide-ranging engagement with simultaneous exchanges of air strikes.

Lt. Comdr. James R. Lee, skipper of Scouting 10, led his wingman in a search to the northwest that morning. He struck pay dirt, as he recalled 30 years later:

"We were at the end of our search, about 200 miles out, and immediately started to climb to get altitude for a bombing attack since we carried 500-pound bombs.

"While climbing, at about 3,500 feet we spotted seven Zeroes above on a parallel course on the starboard beam. They passed ahead rapidly, turned and started an opposite approach. Things happened fast. About the time my plane was hit in the armored windshield with small caliber, I got off a burst of forward .50 caliber at the leading Jap. He exploded as he passed beneath me, narrowly missing colliding.

"Lt. (jg) W. E. Johnson and I jinked around and were able to reach the base of the somewhat sparse cloud cover (around 4,000 feet) where we ducked in and out, still having an attack or at least another good report on the CV doings in mind, but we met the CAP every time we popped out. We finally got separated in these maneuvers, and each made his own way back to *Enterprise* since we had used up a lot of fuel and it seemed pointless to keep up the hide and seek any longer."

While Lee and Johnson played aerial tag with *Shokaku* and *Zuikaku's* CAP, another VS-10 team got in a solid lick. Lt. Stockton B. Strong, an extremely aggressive aviator, stalked the light carrier *Zuiho* with Ens. Charles Irvine. Gaining a favorable position, the two scouts dived on the light carrier and scored a direct hit plus a near miss. They escaped the vengeful Mitsubishis and a cloud of flak to return from an exceptional mission.

Hornet's SBD crews, including many frustrated veterans of Midway, finally got a shot at Japanese carriers. Accurate scouting reports had plotted the location of *Shokaku* and *Zuikaku*, which became the primary target. Leading Bombing Eight was Lt. James "Moe" Vose, who wrote, "Gus Widhelm (commanding Scouting Eight) and I joined our squadrons and passed directly over the Japanese cruiser group and continued on, all the while under Zero attack. Gus was hit in sight of the carriers, and landed almost in the middle of the disposition. During our approach the Zeroes would line up in echelon ahead, and as they peeled off our formation would simply turn into them.

"I was first to dive. Widhelm's people had joined on me, and I saw three hits.

"As we pulled out we were taking evasive action at wave-top level, under continued Zero attack.

"We came in sight of our task force and recognition procedures for an even day were to make left-hand turns, and dip the left wing twice. As we would do so, we would be met by a hail of AA! This is understandable, as the force had been under severe attack, the *Hornet* badly hit, and *Enterprise* on fire forward with a bomb hit aft. On landing, *Enterprise's* after elevator was jammed in the down position and it was necessary to catch the number one wire. I can still recall that yawning hole in the deck.

"When we landed on *Enterprise*, Lt. (jg) Fred Bates, my flight officer, gave me a piece of charred wood from the flight deck of *Shokaku* from my hit! It had blown into his cockpit on his way down."

An *Enterprise* search team also struck *Junyo* in a well-executed attack.

Hornet was mortally wounded, ending her career one year after commissioning. *Enterprise*, though sustaining bomb damage, would fight again—and again.

While Santa Cruz represented a tactical loss for the U.S. Navy, the strategic situation remained unchanged— a *de facto* American victory.

With both sides' carriers removed from the equation, land-based air power again came to prominence. However, repeated bombardments by Japanese battleships caused heavy damage to Henderson Field, and at one point the marines had only a single airworthy SBD. Usually outnumbered and outgunned, American warships engaged in a series of nocturnal surface engagements with enemy battleships, cruisers, and destroyers that resulted in losses to both navies but preserved the status quo.

By mid-November the American and Japanese commands recognized that the bloodletting could not last much longer. Losses of trained personnel, ships, and aircraft were serious enough to force the issue, and the campaign climaxed in the three-day Naval Battle of Guadalcanal.

Though another surface engagement preceded the main event, leading to SBDs and TBFs sinking the stricken battleship *Hiei* on the 13th, the greater threat appeared from the north. A convoy of troop transports and destroyers steamed down The Slot beneath a near-continuous CAP of Zeroes. If the enemy troops landed in

"The indispensable man" was the carriers landing signal officer(LSO). A naval aviator himself, the LSO guided his fellow airmen during the final stages of landing by a standard set of signals he gave with his paddles. Many a wounded, frightened, and/or fatigued pilot owed his life to thje LSO who brought him safely aboard. Lietenant (jg) Walter F. Wujcik works a pilot aboard Bellau Wood (CVL-24) in 1945. *USN photo*

sufficient strength, the balance ashore would tip in Tokyo's favor. Cactus responded with a daylong assault on the transports, thanks in no small part to *Enterprise's* relatively new Air Group 10 shuttling between Henderson Field and The Big E.

"Cactus"-based Dauntlesses sank one cruiser and hit two more, but the focus was upon the transports. The frantic pace of operations precluded normal squadron operations as navy and marine SBD and TBF crews swapped aircraft, led by whomever appeared to be senior.

Scouting Ten skipper "Bucky" Lee recalled the hectic pace of operations, saying, "Henderson Field was really jammed. There was not much time for any maintenance during the operations against the 'Tokyo Express' and indeed not many available maintenance people since Air Group 10 had flown in flight crews only. There was much swapping of planes between pilots; gear was borrowed (somebody got away with my chute), and flights took off composed of navy and marine pilots, led by whoever was senior. Generally, coordination was excellent—though living conditions were something else."

Over the Japanese transports, Wildcats kept most of the Zeroes and floatplanes at bay as Dauntlesses bombed, Avengers released torpedoes, and everybody

with ammunition descended to mast top level to strafe decks packed with Japanese soldiers. Inflicting visible carnage from the air, the operation became known as The Buzzard Brigade—a title that Torpedo Ten proudly carried for the rest of the war.

Throughout the day, Henderson-based aircraft sank six transports, leaving four to put troops ashore.

The unrelenting pattern continued the next day, the 14th, with the most strenuous operational tempo of the campaign. Of a dozen or more Japanese combatant and transport vessels attacked in daylight hours, seven were sunk. Never again would Dauntlesses have so harried or successful a day; never again would Avengers enjoy such easy pickings. When it was over, air crews as well as maintenance and ordnance men slumped in exhaustion.

In early February 1943 the Japanese reversed the "Tokyo Express" and evacuated their last survivors of the Guadalcanal campaign. In the previous six months, U.S.Navy and Marine Corps scout-bombers and torpedo planes had sunk an exceptional variety of enemy ships, including a battleship, a carrier, three cruisers, three destroyers, and at least 14 troop transports. The value of naval strike aircraft had been reinforced beyond all doubt.

CARRIERS IN THE ATLANTIC

Within days of the Naval Battle of Guadalcanal, carrier aviation demonstrated its strategic reach in the Atlantic Theater of Operations. The Allied invasion of French Morocco was designated Operation Torch, supported by four escort carriers and *Ranger* (CV-4) along a 200-mile stretch of coast between Port Lyautey in the north to Safi in the south. Among them, a dozen carrier squadrons operated 36 SBD-3s, 27 TBF-1s, and 109 F4F-4s. They were opposed by a comparable number of French combat aircraft subordinate to army and navy units loyal to the Vichy government in Paris. The situation was ironic in that, technically allied with Nazi Germany, nearly half the Vichy combatant types were of American origin, built by Curtiss, Douglas, and Martin.

Most of the U.S. Navy fliers were "fresh caught" aviators and air crewmen with precious little fleet experience. Their responsibilities for supporting U.S. Army troops included close air support, interdiction, and anti-submarine patrol while the transports offloaded. Vichy naval units in the region included the battleship *Jean Bart*, moored in Casablanca Harbor. Her heavy guns posed a threat to American forces afloat as well as ashore, and *Ranger's* SBDs flew repeated sorties against her on 8 November, first day of Torch. Three French destroyers that sortied from the harbor also were engaged by carrier aircraft and surface ships, and *Suwannee* (ACV-27) bombers sank two submarines in Casablanca Harbor.

While Wildcats fought Vichy's Curtiss Hawks and Dewoitine 520s, SBDs and TBFs were generally unopposed in the air. French antiaircraft fire could be formidable, however, and losses to flak began to mount.

Nevertheless, the need for air support continued unabated. Dauntlesses bombed *Jean Bart* again on the 10th, and all types of carrier planes continued attacking Vichy airfields, troops, and armored forces. *Sangamon's* (ACV-26) Dauntlesses bombed a fort guarding the approach to Port Lyautey so accurately that the garrison surrendered. Aircrews stated during debriefing that the fort resembled the Foreign Legion outpost in the popular film *Beau Geste*!

At the end of Operation Torch's aerial phase, 10 Avengers and 9 Dauntlesses had been lost to all causes, a 30 percent attrition.

Not quite a year later, *Ranger* again launched Dauntlesses and Avengers against Axis ships, but in a far different region from Morocco's desert clime. In October 1943, Operation Leader targeted German-controlled merchant shipping above the Arctic Circle. TBFs of Torpedo Four and SBDs of Bombing Four, flying in the new gray-white Atlantic color scheme, flew two strikes against Bodo, Norway, on the fourth of the month, with *Ranger* escorted by units of the British Home Fleet. Thirty strike sorties were committed, with 20 Dauntlesses delivering the main blow. Two SBDs and a TBFs were downed by German flak gunners, but the dive-bombers and torpedo planes sank five ships and inflicted significant damage on four more.

NORTH FROM "CACTUS"

Following the Guadalcanal campaign, Allied air power raised its sights farther up the Solomons chain. The ultimate goal was Rabaul, the major naval-air complex on New Britain, some 500 nautical miles from "Cactus." With additional U.S. Navy, Marine Corps, Army, and New Zealand squadrons available in early 1943, Commander, Aircraft Solomons Strike (AirSols) conducted a series of operations to neutralize Japanese bases in the central islands while providing air cover for amphibious landings along the way.

Among the many AirSols squadrons at Guadalcanal during 1943 was VB-11, whose parent air group had no carrier. One of the SBD pilots was Lt. (jg) Edwin M. Wilson, who recalled, "Bombing 11 was scheduled to go aboard USS *Hornet* (CV-8) but she was sunk in the Battle of Santa Cruz on 26 October 1942. With no carrier for Air Group 11, our first combat tour was at Guadalcanal flying from Henderson Field from April to August 1943. We made attacks on Japanese bases throughout the Solomon Islands, all the way up to Bougainville. Throughout this tour—and the subsequent one—my rear-seat man was Harry R. Jespersen of San Diego, then an 18-year-old radioman-gunner. He proved to be very sharp, intelligent, and an outstanding radioman and an accurate gunner.

"On 8 May 1943 Japanese destroyers were reported in Blackett Strait, and VB-11 was ordered to attack them. The weather was lousy; when it was my turn to dive I pulled up over the solid overcast and circled for a while. Finally, through a hole in the cloud cover, I saw a destroyer and dove on it. Being the only plane in the area, I saw lots of tracers and holes appearing in my wings. I got a hit on the DD with my 1,000-pound bomb, and as I was pulling out, I saw three loaded landing barges heading for shore.

"Low on the water, I went back and forth strafing the barges with my .50 calibers until I ran out of ammo. Then I circled them so Jespersen could fire his twin .30s at the soldiers who were firing their rifles and pistols at us. We sank one barge and stopped the other two.

"Both out of ammo, we returned to Henderson Field low on fuel and with lots of holes in the plane. One big hole in my port wing made a strange whistling sound. The engine quit, out of fuel, as I was landing.

"That night the coast watcher on Kolombangara reported the main attack did little damage because of the overcast and low clouds, but later a lone plane hit a destroyer which sank, then strafed three barges headed for his island. That the barges did not make it ashore made him very happy! Years later I found out the coast watcher was an Australian, Reginald Evans, and that the DD I sank was *Oyashio*. A couple of months later—on 7 August 1943—Reg Evans saved Lt. Jack Kennedy and his PT boat crew."

Major landings seized the New Georgia group and much of Bougainville by year-end. Consequently, Rabaul came within easy reach of strike and fighter aircraft, and an aerial siege was implemented that made seizure of the enemy base unnecessary. Two carrier raids in November 1943 inflicted substantial damage on Japanese shipping, and by January 1944 the reduction of Rabaul was nearly complete, maintained by AirSols squadrons. Rabaul was left to wither on the vine.

A similar philosophy was applied to the Central Pacific offensive, supported by carrier- and land-based naval aircraft. For example, the Fourth Marine Aircraft Wing's SBD and TBF squadrons were put to good use in reducing bypassed garrisons in the Gilberts and Marshalls, eventually to the point that even antiaircraft fire all but disappeared. Nevertheless, the "milk runs" continued until the end of the war, preventing the industrious Japanese from rebuilding naval or air facilities that could potentially pose a threat in the backwater of the Pacific War.

BIGGER IF NOT BETTER

From late 1942 until late 1943 the typical fleet carrier embarked 36 fighters and bombers, and 18 torpedo planes; however, the composition of those aircraft began to change before the end of 1943. While the TBF Avenger (and its General Motors TBM version) retained a lock on the torpedo mission, new blood arrived in the form of the Curtiss SB2C Helldiver and the Grumman F6F Hellcat.

Intended to replace the Dauntless, the Helldiver suffered a long, painful gestation before reaching combat nearly two years after Pearl Harbor. Helldivers flew their first missions during the Rabaul strikes of November 1943 and over the next eight months gradually replaced Dauntlesses in carrier bomber squadrons, the VS (scout) mission having been absorbed by VB units earlier that year.

Bigger and faster than the Douglas, the new Curtiss proved a maintenance and operational headache. Most dive-bomber pilots assigned to "The Beast" were partial to the SBD, which they had flown in operational training if not in the fleet. However, VB-17 in the new *Essex*-class carrier *Bunker Hill* (CV-17) made the SB2C-1 into a workable combat aircraft, as did most squadrons that followed.

Meanwhile, Avengers proved themselves as well suited to antisubmarine patrol and close air support as they did to antiship missions. With development of the escort aircraft carrier (CVE), an organizational structure emerged in the composite squadron (VC) concept, usually with Wildcat fighters and TBFs or TBMs as the bombers. As a rule, the "baby flattops" trained for close air support in the Pacific and antisubmarine warfare in the Atlantic, but they were versatile enough to perform both tasks in either theater of operations. Eventually almost 10,000 Avengers were produced by Grumman and GM, nearly as many as the combined total of SBDs and SB2Cs. In short, the Avenger made itself indispensable to naval aviation.

One of the most striking demonstrations of the TBF's versatility occurred at Truk Atoll in February 1944. Lt. Comdr. William I. Martin's VT-10 had trained for radar-directed night bombing and proved the concept with a low-level attack on Japanese merchantmen in the large lagoon. For the loss of one aircraft and crew, Torpedo 10 sank or damaged a dozen ships, gaining greater results with less loss than had been achieved in similar daylight missions.

NEW SHIPS

With new aircraft arriving in the fleet, a new generation of ships had been built as well. Chief among them was the long-lived *Essex* (CV-9) class, whose design had been drafted before the war and was updated based on combat experience. The big, handsome ships were 860–878 feet long, displacing more than 27,000 tons, and capable of operating nearly 100 aircraft. Fast and long-ranged, they were the potent muscle behind the Mid-Pacific offensive that kicked off in summer 1943.

Eventually 15 *Essexes* were deployed during World War II, and 9 more subsequently joined the fleet, serving in the Korean and Vietnam Wars with Skyraiders, Skyhawks, and Crusaders in place of Avengers, Helldivers, and Hellcats.

Despite fearsome damage from bombers, *kamikazes*, and some appalling fires, no *Essex*-class ship was ever sunk in three wars.

As much as *Essexes* were needed—especially since the Pearl Harbor debacle, which effectively ended the battleship's supremacy in the U.S. Navy—not even the combined efforts of four shipyards could meet the growing demand from 1943 onward. Consequently, nine *Cleveland* (CL-55) class light cruiser hulls were completed as small carriers, or CVLs. The 10,000-ton hulls were modified with flight decks and small islands. All were commissioned between January and December 1943, the first being *Independence* (CVL-22), which had been laid down as *Amsterdam* (CL-59) in May 1941. Though much

Navy photomates man flight quarter stations during all carrier flight operations. Today's photographers are more apt to be equipped with electronic equipment rather than a 35mm Mitchell motion picture camera such as the one manned by this photographer on board *Wasp* (CV-7) during June 1942. *USN photo*

smaller than the CV-9 ships, the CVLs were capable of more than 30 knots—enough to operate with the Fast Carrier Task Force. The two designs made excellent teammates for the last two years of the war.

While there was no call for fleet carriers in the Atlantic, a crying need existed for yet smaller flattops to combat the U-boat threat. American shipyards met the need with the production of 138 escort carriers (originally ACV then CVEs) between 1941 and 1945, including nearly 40 for the British Navy. Mainly built in four classes, the "jeep" carriers displaced from 7,000 to 12,000 tons empty, steamed at less than 20 knots, and operated approximately 20 aircraft—almost exclusively Wildcats and Avengers. CVEs represented one of the wonders of the industrial age when the entire 55-ship *Casablanca* (CVE-55) class was delivered between 8 July 1943 and 8 July 1944—an incredible production schedule averaging more than one carrier a week! The last of the line, *Munda* (CVE-104) was merely 103 days from keel laying to commissioning. Five CVEs were lost to submarines, *kamikazes*, and surface ships, but the baby flattops provided a tremendous return on their investment, some fighting again off Korea.

To the aviators flying TBFs, SBDs, and SB2Cs, there was little difference in the size of the *Essex*-class flight decks and those of most prewar carriers. It was quite a different situation, however, for Avenger pilots as-

signed to CVL and CVE squadrons. Precision was the name of the game, as described by retired Capt. Roland H. Dale, a wartime squadron and air group commander:

"*Essex*-class flight decks were 147 feet, 6 inches across while CVL decks were one-quarter narrower at 109 feet, 2 inches. It was like comparing a football field with a tennis court!"

"The shorter hull of the CVL pitched more than that of the CVs. In the Gilberts, where we encountered very light winds but had to contend with a large Pacific swell, we had to steam about 30 knots, and that high speed through the water, combined with the large swells, made for a lively deck with many wave offs when the deck was pitching excessively. With the shorter landing area in the CVL you had less margin for error with a pitching deck. As I recall, the actual landing width for catching a wire on a CVL was about 78 feet, which I believe was less than that of the CVEs!"

ROUTINE DANGERS

Combat was often less hazardous than "routine" training flights. VB-11's Lt (jg) Edwin M. Wilson, an SBD pilot recalls a 1943 incident at NAS Barbers Point, Hawaii:

"At 0500 we started taxiing to takeoff position. It was pitch black, with no moon. As they had no runway lights, we squared off on the runway and headed for a red light in the center of the runway at the far end. An Army B-24 that was supposed to simulate a high-level bombing attack on Pearl Harbor took off first. As he became airborne, there was a hell of a white flash and for a second you could read a newspaper in the cockpit. That did not help our night vision!

"The skipper, Lt. Comdr. Weldon Hamilton, was off next. Ens. Ford took off right after him; finally it was Lt. 'Snapper' Knapp's turn. Being his wingman, I was to take off after him. Just as Snapper started his roll, the VT-11 TBFs that were parked on my right side, facing the runway, were starting up. One of them switched on his running lights. Snapper apparently mistook that Avenger's light as the red light at the end of the runway. Consequently, the first TBF chopped off the tip of Snapper's right wing and the second TBF took off more. Snapper boresighted the red running light of the third TBF, and chopped his way through the wing almost up to the fuselage, where he ground to a halt.

The cost of war is always high, and never more costly than when it involves human life. Flight deck crews carry a casualty below on board a Pacific Fleet CVL after a raid in the Gilberts and Marshalls, c. November–December 1943. *USN photo*

"As I was observing all the sparks and flame up ahead, the plane director signaled me to take off. I shook my head in a negative manner. In exasperation, he got up on the wing to tell me to take off immediately. I kept saying, 'Something happened up there and I am not taking off.' Even after threatening me with a court martial, I refused. At that time the word was passed to cut engines and remain in cockpits.

"After what seemed a very long time, the dawn gave enough light to show the runway partially covered by parts of wings, props, and engines. A real mess. My gunner, Radioman Harry Jespersen, was damn glad I had refused to head into that debris. After the runway was cleared, we finally took off.

"On our return to Barbers Point, Ensign Pickering could not lower his port wheel, so he was told to land wheels up after burning most of his fuel. This gave plenty of time for the word to spread all over the air station than an SBD was going to land wheels up. This news brought everyone out of the woodwork to line the runway, including us. No naval aviator ever played to a larger house. He landed O.K., with the cheers of many applauding him.

"We later learned that the big white flash we had seen was caused by the B-24 when it crashed into the water just after taking off from Barking Sands. Fortunately, 9 of the 12 men aboard survived."

During the first half of 1944, the workhorse SBD remained a major player in the naval air war. In the six months from December 1943 to June 1944, the number of Dauntless squadrons in the Pacific increased to a total of 31, including 11 marine units. Fifteen of the navy SBD squadrons were land-based VS units providing local patrols for bases from Hawaii to the Marshalls, but their carrier-borne counterparts still had a part to play on the global stage.

The Avenger also was continually heard from, and announced itself to the Japanese in an innovative fashion early one morning. During a *Yorktown* predawn strike against Marcus Island the skipper of VT-5, Lt. Comdr. Richard Upson, broke formation. Making a solo approach to the enemy field, he turned on his landing lights and in the words of another *Yorktowner*, "made a rather normal approach to the runway." Consequently, he received a green light from the control tower and obliged the duty watch by bombing the runway and the tower! The rest of Air Group Five followed suit, to the considerable consternation of the Japanese.

BATTLE OFF THE MARIANAS

By the time of the Marianas operation in June 1944, a big-deck air group typically flew 40 fighters, 32 Dauntlesses or Helldivers, and 18 Avengers. The *Independence*-class CVLs nominally operated 24 F6F and 9 TBMs, for a Task Force 58 total of 174 Helldivers, 55 Dauntlesses, and 194 Avengers deployed in 15 fast carriers. Another 83 TBFs and TBMs flew from 8 escort carriers providing antisubmarine patrol and close air support.

There had been no carrier battles since the Santa Cruz engagement of October 1942, but American possession of the Marianas—1,500 miles from Japan—was a threat that Tokyo could not ignore. Consequently, nine Imperial Navy flattops with 439 aircraft sortied to oppose the amphibious assault of Saipan, resulting in the largest carrier engagement ever fought.

Actually, the disparity in air power was not as great as the carrier numbers would suggest. Approximately 600 Japanese naval aircraft were available from bases on Saipan, Guam, and Tinian, but coordination proved erratic, and the general state of Japanese training was poor. Previous attrition, especially in the Solomons, had eroded the qualitative edge that Imperial Navy squadrons possessed in the first year of the Pacific War.

On the morning of 19 June, Task Force 58 search teams fanned out to seek the Japanese carriers previously reported by American submarines. Scouting doctrine had evolved from the early days of 1942 when typically two SBDs scoured a wedge-shaped search sector. Now, with far more aircraft available, each team generally comprised two Avengers or Helldivers escorted by one Hellcat. Reconnaissance was the primary objective, but if any team found Vice Adm. Jisaburo Ozawa's carriers, after sending a contact report, the TF 58 planes were to attack with bombs and torpedoes in hope of damaging at least one enemy flattop.

Each search sector was 315 nautical miles outbound with a 75-mile cross leg before returning to "Point Option" where Vice Admiral Mitscher's task force was expected. However, Ozawa kept his three units beyond effective scouting range and the searchers returned without sighting their quarry. In the meantime, Ozawa's long-range attackers found Mitscher—and were destroyed in the process.

During the day four Japanese air strikes assailed Task Force 58. Hellcat pilots eagerly pounced on the raiders, splashing more than 300 near TF 58 or over Japanese bases at Guam and Saipan. Additionally, U.S. submarines sank two of Ozawa's nine carriers, and by dusk he was retiring westward, thoroughly beaten. American losses were 30 carrier aircraft to all causes, including 12 dive-bombers and torpedo planes.

Searches continued throughout the next day, but not until late afternoon of 20 June was the Japanese Mobile Fleet accurately plotted. Consequently, Task Force 58 launched 227 planes against Ozawa, including 51 Helldivers, 54 Avengers, and 26 Dauntlesses. It was a long chase—300 miles outbound—which guaranteed a return to the task force after dark.

Some 250 miles outbound a Japanese refueling group was sighted, trailing the carriers by 40 to 50 miles. Wasp's Air Group attacked the support force, sinking two oilers and damaging a third. Despite the success, however, Air Group 14 sustained heavy losses: 11 of 12 Helldivers and 3 of 7 Avengers shot down or lost in water landings en route back to the task force. It was an ill omen of things to come on "the mission beyond darkness."

Ozawa's three carrier units were attacked by portions of six U.S. air groups that largely shot their way through the Japanese combat air patrol. Some 20 TF-58 planes were shot down over the enemy fleet, but the others pressed their attacks.

None were more aggressive than the torpedo pilots of Belleau Wood's VT-24. Lt. George Brown's four-plane division went for the new carrier Hiyo, though one pilot diverted to attack a CVL. Brown led his other two wingmen through heavy, accurate flak. Said Lt. (jg) Warren Omark, "We fanned out to approach from different angles. The attack course took us over the outlying screen of destroyers, then cruisers, and finally the battleships. This screen had to be penetrated in order to reach the proper range for launching torpedoes against the carrier. The antiaircraft fire was very intense and I took as much evasive action as I could."

During the low-level approach, Brown's TBF was set afire, forcing his radioman and gunner to bail out. Brown pressed his attack, launched his torpedo, and egressed through the screening vessels. So did Omark and Lt. (jg) Benjamin Tate. They rejoined Brown on a homeward heading but soon lost sight of his blackened, flak-damaged TBF in the gathering dusk. Brown received a posthumous Navy Cross for his heroism; his air crewmen were rescued the following day.

Hiyo, a handsome 24,000-ton ship, took one or more torpedo hits and sank that night. TorpRon 24 had proved the validity of the TBF and the U.S. Navy's aerial torpedo capability, as no other Japanese warship was sunk wholly by carrier-based torpedo attack.

Yorktown (CV-10) and Hornet (CV-12) squadrons concentrated on the largest enemy ship, Zuikaku, which had launched against Pearl Harbor and fought at Coral Sea as well as Santa Cruz. SB2C and TBF pilots claimed several hits, though the Japanese insisted she was struck by just one bomb with six others assessed as near misses. Bunker Hill (CV-17) aviators went after light carrier Chiyoda, while Enterprise and Lexington's formations divided their attention between two of Ozawa's task groups. Junyo and Chiyoda both were hit, while CVL Ryuho took some near misses. Additionally, a battleship and cruiser were attacked with moderate results.

In the darkening sky, by squadrons and singles, American aircraft turned eastward. Radio discipline often fell apart as pilots asked the most direct heading for

TF 58 while others announced they were ditching, out of fuel. The YE-ZB homer transmitting from each carrier helped steer some planes to safety, but many lacked the fuel to climb high enough to receive the beacon. Others relied on radar, including ARM1/c David Cawley, flying with Lieutenant Lt. Comdr. of *Enterprise's* Bombing Ten.

"I concentrated on our radar, which had a maximum range of 75 miles," Cawley related. "Our ship could send a homing signal that we could receive on the radar. At 90 miles this signal began to show clearly in the pitch dark. We adjusted course only a few degrees and continued on. It was about 2030 and lots of planes were going in the water, out of gas, and some landing together in sections and divisions. The radio was chaos."

Approaching "The Big E," Ramage and Cawley saw that the deck was fouled with a crashed airplane. With no fuel to spare, they recovered aboard *Yorktown* and gladly remained as "guests" overnight.

Total strike aircraft losses amounted to 29 of 54 Avengers; 43 of 51 Helldivers; but only 4 of 26 Dauntlesses. The large majority were noncombat-related losses, fuel exhaustion, and deck crashes being the two greatest causes. In its final fleet action that reliable old warhorse, the SBD, had again proved itself the class of the field. However, Dauntless production ended the following month and carrier bombing squadrons were stuck with the SB2C, for better or worse.

Fortunately, better was on the way. The SB2C-3, much improved over the dash one, was described by retired Vice Admiral Donald Engen, a junior *Lexington* aviator in 1944:

"The SB2C-3 was an entirely different airplane than the dash ones that we had flown earlier. The bigger engine, and the electric governed four-bladed propeller gave it much more power." Pilots also approved of the simplified hydraulic system, as did hard-working maintenance men who had endured countless headaches fighting "the Beast" in its original form. The SB2C-3 fully equipped the eight Fast Carrier Force VB squadrons in time for the next campaign.

THE PHILIPPINES

In August 1944, prior to the Philippines campaign, an upgrade to 54 Hellcats per *Essex*-class carrier forced further reductions to 24 Helldivers while 18 Avengers

were retained. Complements aboard light and escort carriers were little changed, nominally 9 TBMs per CVL torpedo squadron and CVE composite squadron.

The 20 October landing of U.S. Army troops on Leyte guaranteed a response from the Imperial Navy, still stinging from its mauling off the Marianas four months before. A typically complex Japanese plan sought to concentrate widespread fleet units against the Leyte beaches, but American submarine and aerial reconnaissance detected each segment in turn. On 24 October Vice Adm. Marc Mitscher's carrier task groups began hammering 33 enemy warships in the Sibuyan and Sulu Seas. Overflying the islands of Leyte and Samar from the east, the Task Force 38 air groups found more hostile tonnage than most of the aviators had ever seen.

Chief among the targets were the twin sisters *Yamato* and *Musashi*, 63,000-ton battleships boasting huge, 18-inch guns. Strike directors, usually the senior air group commander from each task group, concentrated their attacks upon *Musashi* and gradually wore her down. For most of the SB2C and TBF crews, it was a five and a half hour round-trip mission. While 10 Helldivers and 11 Avengers were lost, the huge majority of the hundreds of sorties safely returned to their ships. A Japanese cruiser also was sunk, and Vice Adm. Takeo Kurita's force was seen to reverse helm late that afternoon. The western threat to General MacArthur's landing beaches seemed neutralized.

Perhaps of equal importance to the aviators, *Musashi*—one of the largest ships ever built up to that time—had been sunk entirely by carrier aircraft. The battleship clearly had been supplanted by the carrier, with its strike aircraft, as the capital ship of the twentieth century.

While the fast carriers dealt with Kurita, land-based Japanese naval aviation inflicted a loss on TF 38. The light carrier *Independence*, name ship of her class, was set ablaze by a single bomb hit and had to be abandoned. At sunset on the 24th, however, the ledger showed strongly in favor of the U.S. Third Fleet.

At dawn on 25 October the Seventh Fleet—"MacArthur's Navy," so named for its amphibious support role—had escort carrier groups steaming off Samar to assist the troops ashore. Then a patrolling Avenger noted strange ships with pagoda masts emerging from the east end of San Bernardino Strait. During the night, Kurita had regrouped his armada and, with

In February 1942, the navy established a new aircraft maintenance program based on land-based Carrier Air Service Units (CASUs) and ship-based Carrier Air Service Divisions (CASDs). The CASUs precluded the necessity of carrier squadrons sending maintenance personnel ashore when aircraft required maintenance off the ship. CASDs assisted the squadrons at sea. Maintenance personnel work here on a VT-5 TBF-1 on board *Yorktown* (CV-10) about late 1943. *USN photo*

Yamato intact, transited the waters between Luzon and Samar. Though night-flying TBMs from *Independence* tracked him, the word eluded Third Fleet's Adm. William F. Halsey, and Kurita caught the Americans completely by surprise.

That was bad enough, but Halsey had learned of four Japanese carriers well to the north and pursued them with his characteristic aggressiveness. Consequently, his prime weapons—9 squadrons of dive-bombers and 16 torpedo squadrons of Task Force 38—were hopelessly out of position to counter the unexpected threat.

Square in the path of nearly 30 enemy ships was the escort carrier group of Rear Adm. Clifton Sprague. Six CVEs with a handful of destroyers and destroyer escorts were all that stood in Kurita's way. Once past "Taffy Three,"

the Japanese would have easy pickings among the Seventh Fleet transport ships offloading supplies for the army.

Throughout the morning, composite squadrons from Sprague's *Casablanca*-class CVEs threw themselves at Kurita's battleships and cruisers. Fortunately, two more "Taffies" were within tactical radius of Sprague's command, as Grumman and Eastern aircraft fought desperately to save the outgunned, outnumbered, and outsped escort carriers. One senior aviator, Lt. Comdr. Ed Huxtable of *Gambier Bay's* (CVE-73) VC-10, coordinated with his Annapolis classmate, Comdr. Richard Fowler of *Kitkun Bay's* (CVE-71) VC-5, to mix up "dry" and "wet" runs by Avengers and Wildcats, as the Japanese had no way of knowing which aircraft carried bombs or torpedoes and which did not. Many pilots launched with nothing but machine gun ammunition, as there was no time to load ordnance under battleship or cruiser shell fire.

Eventually the enemy's superiority began to tell. *Gambier Bay* and three escorts succumbed to close-range cruiser guns; others were damaged. But the aviators fought back persistently, sinking three of Kurita's cruisers. Disheartened, the Japanese admiral assumed he had stumbled onto a fast carrier task group and disengaged. Taffy Three—and the invasion beachhead—were saved.

Steaming with Taffy Two aboard *Marcus Island* (CVE-77) was Lt. Comdr. T. O. Murray's VC-21. The squadron diarist commented:

"We learned that the Japanese Fleet had crossed San Bernardino Strait and was attacking a CVE unit just north of us. In fact, some components of the fleet were also attacking *us*! You could see the enemy ships on the horizon from the bridge, and large geysers of water near our destroyer screen indicated the Japs' effort to get a few of us, too.

"The saddest sight the pilots witnessed during the entire attack was the expression on the skipper's face when he learned that all but three of our torpedoes had been given to planes of the other ships before we could return from our mission. His greatest ambition was to take his torpedo squadron in on a coordinated attack. To suddenly find there were no torpedoes available must have been a great letdown. Two pilots from another ship were ready to go with two of the torpedoes, and the skipper insisted upon taking the remaining one. Except for two of our pilots, this was the first torpedo attack for the rest of Twenty-One.

"Our planes joined with those of other ships in our unit and the flight, led by Lt. Comdr. J. R. Dale of VC-20, went after the Japs. During this attack our skipper scored a hit on the stern of a heavy cruiser that went dead in the water. It was on this particular attack that the enemy fleet was diverted from their original course. They were forced to take a heading of north, and reached a position a little northeast of Samar Island before we caught up with them again.

"When the boys returned from the first attack they delayed only long enough to gulp down some coffee and sandwiches while their planes were being re-gassed and re-armed. The skipper led this flight of planes to the target. A beautiful, coordinated attack was made with excellent results. At this time the enemy was desperately trying to gain the protective water of San Bernardino Strait."

On the return flight to Taffy Two, Commander Murray's division was jumped by three Tonys, which pressed an attack on the torpedo planes. Maneuvering close to the water, to say nothing of four eager turret gunners, soon discouraged the Ki-61 pilots.

Meanwhile, far to the north, closing on Vice Admiral Ozawa's carriers off Cape Engano, Task Force 38 was determined to end Japan's naval air power capability forever. Three task groups dealt with the carriers, while the fourth reversed course to succor the CVEs.

Essex and *Lexington* aircraft were first overhead Ozawa, sinking a light carrier. Bombing 19 pilots described the flak as "the most concentrated AA fire yet seen," with 19 Helldivers and 11 Avengers lost to all causes throughout the day. Repeated strikes whittled down the Imperial Navy's remaining flight decks, including *Zuikaku*, which had fought every carrier battle except Coral Sea. Light carriers *Chitose*, *Chiyoda*, and *Zuiho* also were sunk in the course of 587 TF 38 sorties against Ozawa.

To the south, Task Group 38.2 (*Intrepid*, *Hancock*, *Cabot*, and *Independence*) pursued Kurita's battered surface force, harrying *Yamato* and her consorts back through the San Bernardino Strait. Over the next two days naval aviators sank another cruiser and four destroyers.

Though two-thirds of the Japanese ships escaped the Battle of Leyte Gulf, Tokyo was finished as a naval power, having lost four carriers, three battleships, nine cruisers, and eight destroyers—a small fleet in itself.

While the Emperor's warships failed to inflict serious losses on the Americans, his aviators were more

successful. The debut of the Special Attack Corps was a frightful success from the U.S. Navy's perspective, as suicide aircraft sank *St. Lô* (CVE-63) and damaged six more escort carriers.

TO NIPPON'S SHORE

The *kamikaze* crisis of late 1944 resulted in yet another expansion of carrier fighter strength. In November, 73 fighters were allotted *Essex*-class carriers; the increased strength formalized with the establishment of fighter-bomber squadrons in January 1945. Something had to give, and it was bombers. TorpRons were reduced to 12 or 15 Avengers, while some SB2C squadrons were "beached" and VB pilots began checking out in F6Fs. In some air groups, pilots flew fighters and dive-bombers alternately. The rationale was irrefutable, as fighters could double as dive-bombers, but Avengers were needed for torpedo attack and antisubmarine patrol.

In early 1945 Allied forces inexorably drew nearer their ultimate target: Japan itself. The seizure of Iwo Jima in the Bonins, only 750 miles south of Tokyo, placed the enemy capital in range of Seventh Air Force land-based fighters. Meanwhile, major strikes were flown by Task Force 58, penetrating weather fronts over the enemy home islands in mid-February and mid- to late March.

DIVE-BOMBERS IN DECLINE

Throughout the war years, U.S. Navy acceptances of carrier strike aircraft increased considerably: from nearly 6,000 during 1943 to almost 8,000 the following year. However, barely 5,000 were delivered in the shortened year of 1945, which indicated not only the end of the war but the growing importance of carrier-based fighters. From near parity with strike aircraft in 1943, fighters easily outstripped dive-bombers and torpedo planes in 1944: 12,041 to 7,821, or about 50 percent more fighters. The disparity was somewhat greater in 1945: 8,269 to 5,015, or 1.6 fighters for each carrier-capable attack aircraft.

The reason for increasing fighter emphasis, of course, was the greater need for fleet air defense—in a word, *kamikazes*. Combined with the fact that fighters could effectively deliver bombs and rockets, the decline in emphasis of attack aircraft was both necessary and inevitable.

By January 1945 the *kamikazes* had forced a serious rethinking of fast carrier organization. First encountered in the Philippines three months before, Japan's suicide squadrons mandated more fighters aboard U.S. and British carriers, which meant something had to give. The obvious solution was to reduce SB2Cs in favor of TBFs, which already were delivering more ordnance than Helldivers. Therefore, in January TBFs and TBMs carried 62 percent of the fast carriers' bomb loads compared to barely 16 percent for the Helldiver. The balance, some 22 percent, was carried by fighter-bombers; primarily F6Fs.

THE NIGHT BUSINESS

Following *Independence's* successful cruise with Night Air Group 41 under Comdr. Turner Caldwell, in January 1945 Comdr. Bill Martin returned to *Enterprise* as skipper of a dedicated night air group. His pilots included several Torpedo 10 veterans, including an irreverent, aggressive TBM pilot, Lt. Charles "Hotshot Charlie" Henderson. With typical enthusiasm he recalled the hectic period:

"Bill Martin's dream had come true. He had Night Air Group 90 aboard a night carrier—the Big E again—with our very own special task group. The only problem was, they didn't want us to fly at night! After we got shot up in daylight, several of us considered landing in China after 'severe AA damage to our aircraft over the target.' Anything would have been an improvement!

"We had received our new aircraft (TBM-3E Avengers) at Barbers Point, Hawaii, a week before flying aboard The Big E. During that time we incorporated about 100 changes, including stripping thousands of pounds of useless hardware: the splendid turrets, tunnel gun, oxygen system, etc. Later BuAer was aghast to learn that our center of gravity was 9 inches forward of the allowable limit—on an aircraft which had to land tail down to catch a wire with the hook!

"'Ground them' BuAer telexed frantically. But by that time we had done hundreds of landings and had no problems.

"We now had an efficient night carrier aircraft with innovative systems aboard ship. Lt. Bill Chase, who flew with Commander Martin, organized radar tracking of our TBMs on our downwind leg and told us when to turn. Thus, we always arrived at the aft port quarter of the flight deck, in perfect formation for the LSO to do his stuff. It was safer and easier than a day landing, as we demonstrated to Vice Admiral Mitscher's considerable surprise.

"We also improved our tactics. Single plane missions were normal, with no wingman. Wingmen often developed vertigo trying to fly formation at night. No longer did we waste time and fuel on rendezvous. We learned to drop flares and get a bearing to determine wind for navigation on long missions. We could carry four 500-pound bombs, eight rockets, flares, and droppable fuel tanks to range over 400 miles from base with several hours on target. Lt. Jim Plummer radically improved our radar performance—over 50 miles for ships and 15 miles for aircraft.

"After wasting a lot of time, men, and equipment with Admiral Halsey and with morale at a low ebb (we lost two planes and crews to 'friendly' AA fire) we finally settled into the Iwo/Chichi Jima-Okinawa-Japan routine. It was still more day than night flying, but we had not volunteered for dangerous day missions! We were most resentful."

Eventually the resentment dissipated as Commander Martin aggressively pushed for more nocturnal missions. By the time the air group's deployment ended in May, his night bombers and fighters were an integral part of "The Big Blue Blanket" that covered Japanese airfields and coastal shipping routes round the clock.

OKINAWA AND BEYOND

The last major campaign of the war was Operation Iceberg, the invasion of the Ryukyus. During the last week of March, 18 CVEs of Rear Adm. Cal Durgin's escort carrier group launched preliminary strikes against Kerama Retto and Okinawa itself. In May they were joined by the first two Marine Corps air groups aboard *Block Island* (CVE-106) and *Gilbert Islands* (CVE-107), with two more reaching the Western Pacific before VJ-Day. Besides Corsairs and Hellcats, each group operated a dozen Avengers for antisub patrol, strike, and close air support for the "mud marines."

Vice Admiral Mitscher's Task Force 58 brought 10 big-deck carriers and six CVLs to Operation Iceberg, the largest concentration of carrier air power yet achieved. Only 300 nautical miles from southern Kyushu, Okinawa was the last steppingstone to the Home Islands, and the Japanese resisted with—literally—suicidal fury. L-Day was Sunday, 1 April, simultaneously Easter and April Fools' Day.

The greatest *kamikaze* of all was the battleship *Yamato*, which had escaped carrier aviators less than six months previously in the Philippines. On 7 April the huge ship, attended by nine escorts, set course for Okinawa with the intention of shelling the landing beaches. Detected in worsening weather, the small armada received the undivided attention of Task Force 58.

During the day, some 380 sorties were flown against the *Yamato* group—about as many as six Japanese carriers had launched against Pearl Harbor. Low ceilings prevented four SB2C squadrons from making standard dive-bombing attacks, but repeated hits were claimed on the warships maneuvering on a spume-flecked ocean beneath leaden skies. Avengers put as many as 19 torpedoes into the 63,000-ton dreadnought, while Helldivers, Hellcats, and Corsairs added bombs and rockets to the ordnance tonnage. A light cruiser and four destroyers went to the bottom in another inevitable but convincing display of the superiority of naval aviation over conventional warships. One destroyer sank in as little as three minutes of being hit; *Yamato* succumbed to repeated bombs and torpedoes after an hour and 40 minutes. The day's events went into the books as the Battle of the East China Sea.

Destruction of *Yamato* and her screen was not achieved without loss. Task Force 58 reported 10 planes lost on the mission including 4 SB2C and 3 TBMs, though 5 additional Avengers were jettisoned from their carriers, too badly damaged to bother with repair.

The British Royal Navy also flew TBMs, with five squadrons of Avenger Is and IIs flying with the British Pacific Fleet, which operated as Task Force 57 alongside Task Force 58. The Fleet Air Arm Avengers shared deck space with Fairey Barracuda dive-bombers and Firefly strike fighters in suppressing Japanese bases in the Sakishimas and Formosa before concluding operations over Japan itself.

Okinawa was declared secure on 21 June, by which time many air groups had been engaged in continuous operations for more than two months. The record was held by *Essex's* Air Group 83 with 79 straight days of combat operations against Okinawa and the Home Islands.

Following the conclusion of Operation Iceberg, the fast carriers raised their sights exclusively toward Japan. With the Fifth Fleet/Third Fleet switch, beginning 10 July, Vice Adm. John S. McCain's Task Force 38 launched strikes the length and breadth of the enemy homeland, from Kyushu in the south to Hokkaido in the north. Alternating between the Tokyo Plain and

coastal areas, Avengers and Helldivers expended bombs, torpedoes, and rockets on a wide variety of targets, including merchant shipping and combatant vessels. Carrier aviators claimed 23 Japanese warships sunk or destroyed in the five-week period preceding Tokyo's acceptance of the Allied surrender demand on 15 August. By that time the fuel-starved Imperial Navy—or what remained of it—was largely bottled up in Kure Harbor and a few other ports.

At the end, Task Force 38 deployed an awesome array of air power, including 9 squadrons of SB2Cs and 16 of TBM. Two attacks were airborne on the morning of the 15th: 103 planes in "Strike Able" and 73 more in "Strike Baker." Word came of Tokyo's capitulation just as the first squadrons crossed the coast, prompting Helldivers and Avengers to turn back, jettison ordnance, and return to the task force. Hellcats and Corsairs tangled with Japanese interceptors throughout the day, but by early afternoon the shooting was over.

A few of the pilots airborne over Japan that day had flown and fought their way across the Pacific in the cockpits of dive-bombers and torpedo planes. Leading VF-86 in *Wasp* (CV-18) was Lt. Comdr. Cleo J. Dobson, who as an *Enterprise* SBD pilot had survived the Sunday surprise at Pearl Harbor 45 months before. At the head of Torpedo 86, still flying "torpeckers," was Lt. Comdr. L. F. Steffenhagen, a TBD veteran of the Coral Sea battle, while Lt. Comdr. Stockton B. Strong of the Eastern Solomons and Santa Cruz had traded his Dauntless for a Corsair in *Shangri-La* (CV-38).

The path to Tokyo Bay had been long and sanguinary. But attack aviators and air crews could report back home: mission accomplished.

THE ORDNANCE WAR

Strike aircraft naturally required ordnance, and the navy equipped its attack squadrons with a marvelous variety. From machine guns to acoustic homing torpedoes to powerful rockets, naval aviators and air crewmen employed every weapon available against Axis targets on land, at sea, and in the air.

Among carrier aircraft, none carried so diverse a battery of aviation ordnance as the TBF/TBM Avenger. Equipped with a horizontal bomb sight, it could perform capably against fixed positions such as island defenses, and of course the TBF owned a monopoly in the torpedo attack role. From 1942 through 1945, U.S. carrier aircraft expended 1,311 aerial torpedoes in the Pacific Theater of Operations. Excluding some 60 Mark 13s carried by TBDs in the first half of 1942, Avengers owned the VT mission throughout the war. Navy records show 131 torpedoes expended in combat during 1942; 116 in 1943; a sensational 772 in 1944; and 292 during 1945.

After Midway, Pacific Fleet torpedo squadrons realized that position relative to the target was crucial with the Mark 13. Summarized VT-6, "The point of dropping must be at a target angle no greater than 70 degrees on either bow and at a range of approximately 800 yards." Torpedo skippers cautioned that any drop that became a trailing shot or stern chase had little chance of a hit.

However, Avengers could and did "haul the mail" with all manner of other naval ordnance: bombs from 250 to 2,000 pounds; incendiaries; depth charges; napalm canisters; mines; and aerial rockets.

High-Velocity Aerial Rockets (HVARs) were widely employed by carrier aircraft from January 1944 onward. During the next 20 months, carrier aviators fired 182,569 HVARs in combat, with the huge majority logged by Hellcats, Wildcats, and Corsairs. TBFs or TBMs fired 55,568, or 30 percent of the total, while SB2Cs seldom used the futuristic weapons: 4,578 or barely 2 percent of the carrier aircraft consumption. Though they could be effective against some ships, more than 90 percent of HVARs were almost exclusively employed against land targets.

As the nature of the war changed, so did the use of naval aircraft. In the 12 months following Pearl Harbor, U.S. Navy and Marine Corps squadrons devoted nearly half their total combat sorties to antishipping missions—either against warships or enemy merchant vessels. That figure was never remotely approached during the rest of the war, as the Coral Sea, Midway, and Guadalcanal campaigns all were fought with combatant and merchant shipping central to the effort.

In the four carrier battles of 1942, both the U.S. and Japanese Navies relied heavily upon dive-bombers as their principal weapons. Aichi D3As scored 70 percent of the hits on American carriers while Nakajima B5Ns achieved 30 percent of the Imperial Navy's total hits on three U.S. carriers.

The American ratio was similar, but more reliant upon SBDs to kill carriers. Approximately 83 percent of the hits on enemy flattops made by U.S. aviators were bombs dropped by Dauntlesses, whereas TBDs and TBFs achieved about 17 percent. The difference, of course, was attributable to the poor quality of aerial torpedoes with which America entered the war: a handicap that made things difficult to impossible for "torpecker" crews. In short, the Imperial Navy's aerial torpedo capability proved twice as effective as its enemy counterpart.

During 1943 the focus shifted to neutralizing Japanese island bases, and fewer than 13 percent of offensive sorties targeted naval or maritime targets. A dramatic upswing in 1944 nearly doubled the 1943 figure, largely owing to the Marianas and Philippines campaigns. However, in the eight combat months of 1945, with Japan's Navy largely sunk or bottled up and her merchant marine crippled, the antishipping figure remained barely above 1943 levels. From 1942 through 1945, only 18.8 percent of carrier aircraft sorties were launched against enemy ships—an ironic situation for the greatest naval war ever waged on planet Earth, but proof of the power projection role of carrier aviation.

The *Essex*-class *Franklin* (CV-13) was heavily damaged by explosions set off on her hangar and flight decks by bombs from two Japanese aircraft off Kyushu, 19 March 1945. Survival after the severe damage sustained by *Franklin* and her sister ship *Bunker Hill* (CV-17) attest to the design quality of the class, as well as the determination and perseverance of their crews. Above right: Amazingly, *Franklin* steamed under her own power to New York Naval Shipyard for repairs following her attack. *USN photo*

Patrol Bombers

During the Second World War the U.S. Navy made extensive use of flying boats and land-based bombers. Generically, they were designated patrol bombers (VPB), capable of performing the separate but related missions of long-range reconnaissance and heavy attack. They were built in comparable numbers, and the navy bought some 4,500 land-based patrol bombers and nearly 4,000 seaplanes (VP) between 1936 and 1945.

In December 1941 the navy owned 466 VP aircraft, the most widely produced being Consolidated's versatile PBY Catalina, a long-range flying boat operated by 21 patrol squadrons. First flown as the XP3Y-1 in early 1935, the "Cat" entered squadron service as the PBY-1 late the following year. The new designation reflected the mission shift from pure patrol to a combined offensive capability. With a 10-year production run in six models, 2,387 Consolidateds were built, plus nearly 700 more

PBY-5A 31-P-9 of VP-31 just prior to departure on a patrol mission from Nas Norfolk in late 1942 or early 1943. *USN photo courtesy of Stan Piet*

In December 1941, the navy was flying 466 patrol bombers (VPB). Consolidated's versatile PBY Catalina was the most widely produced type. The long-range (2,000 miles) flying boat was operated by 21 patrol squadrons. PBY-5 off the East Coast, c. 1941. *Rudy Arnold, courtesy Stan Piet*

First flown as the XP3Y-1 15 March 1935, the "Cat" entered service with VP-11F in October 1936. Before its retirement from operational service with VP-32 in 1949, the patrol bomber was modified into at least 10 versions, such as the PBY-5A amphibian model with retractable landing gear. *USN photo, courtesy Stan Piet*

from Boeing (PB2B), the Naval Aircraft Factory (PBN), and Vickers Canada (OA-10). The PBY-1 through -5 were pure flying boats, while the -5A model received tricycle landing gear. The U.S. Army Air Force's OA-10 also was an amphibian for maximum versatility in the search and rescue role.

Possessed of exceptional range (more than 2,000 miles), the Catalina cruised at a sedate 90 to 100 knots with two Pratt & Whitney R-1830s. Apart from defensive armament of machine guns, its offensive payload included bombs, depth charges, rockets, or torpedoes. In service the PBY proved a rugged, re-liable aircraft, and innovative as well. Consolidated engineers provided retractable wingtip floats that eliminated the drag of conventional fixed floats on most seaplanes of the era.

If any seaplane fought a global war in that global conflict, it was the Catalina. PBYs served in every theater of operation, from the Pacific to the Atlantic and the Mediterranean to the Indian Ocean. Foreign use was exceptional, including the British Commonwealth, Holland, and the Soviet Russia.

Catalinas were flown by RAF Coastal Command to supplement homegrown patrol bombers such as the Short Sunderland. With the U-boat menace barely abated from the "happy time" that the wolf packs enjoyed in 1940, early the following year PBYs were fighting President Franklin Roosevelt's illicit naval war in the North Atlantic. Despite official American neutrality in the European war, U.S. Navy ships and aircraft prosecuted offensive actions against Hitler's navy, and PBYs were involved. In fact, an American-flown Catalina located the battleship *Bismarck* following her spectacular breakout from Norwegian waters and the sinking of HMS *Hood* in May 1941. Acting on that information, Royal Navy aircraft torpedoed the German battleship, slowing her until heavy surface forces arrived to complete the kill.

From early 1942, U.S. Navy PBY were increasingly involved in the Battle of the Atlantic. Flying from Allied bases in Newfoundland, Iceland, and Great Britain, patrol squadrons and wings (PatRons and PatWings) covered the crucial convoy routes to the limit of aircraft range and endurance. With occupation of French Morocco at year's end, the eastern end of the theater also was covered to Casablanca and Port Lyautey.

Eventually, as bases and units were added, the PatWings gained the advantage. Technical innovations such as radar, magnetic anomaly detectors, and specific antisubmarine weapons improved the vulnerable merchant convoys' aerial protection.

U.S. Navy acceptances of PBY Catalinas and the Naval Aircraft Factory version, PBN Nomads, peaked at 592 in 1943, or nearly 50 per month. Thereafter, newer patrol planes were obtained in larger numbers, but the Catalina remained in production until the last PBY-6A was delivered in September 1945.

Other flying boats also made significant contributions to the U-boat war. Martin's gull-winged, twin-engine PBM Mariner was produced from 1939 to 1949, with nearly 1,400 delivered in that decade, beginning in September 1940. Some 10,000 pounds heavier than the PBY, the Mariner was faster, especially in the "dash five"

One model of the PBY was produced for the Army Air Forces as the OA-10A used for air-sea rescue "Dumbo" missions. The OA-10As were built under contract by Canadian Vickers, Ltd., which built Catalinas for the navy under the designation PBV-1A. *Author's coll.*

The Catalina flew a global war, serving in every theater of operation from the Pacific to the Atlantic. Catalinas fought in the Aleutians as well as the Mediterranean and Indian Oceans. Here, PBY-5A of Patrol Wing 4 is over the Aleutians in 1943. *USN photo*

On 10 June 1942, PatWing 4 PBYs discovered the presence of Japanese invasion troops on the islands of Kiska and Attu in the Aleutian chain. VB-135 or -136 PBY-5As and Lockheed PV-1 Venturas are at an advance base in the Aleutians, c. mid-1943. *USN photo*

Undoubtedly the most renowned PBY units were the "Black Cat" squadrons that fought bombing and torpedo missions against Japanese shipping for three years in the Pacific. This VP-52 PBY-5 Cat shows the wear and tear of its combat missions on its black paint scheme during a 10 February 1944 flight. *USN photo*

Consolidated's PB2Y Coronado was used in a variety of roles. In addition to its patrol bomber duties, it served in medical evacuation, transport, and flagship roles.
A PB2Y-3 in flight, c. 1943.
USN photo, courtesy Hal Andrews

Under a July 1942 agreement with the AAF, the navy began acquisition of Consolidated B-24D Liberator bombers and designated them PB4Y-1. Transitional training squadrons began receiving the aircraft in August and VP-51, the first operational unit, accepted its initial Liberator in October. An England-based PB4Y-1 in Atlantic camouflage is caught over the Bay of Biscay, c. mid-1943. *USN photo*

model with two of Pratt & Whitney's superb R-2800 radials rated at 2,000 horsepower.

Wartime production of the Mariner was remarkably consistent, with 317 PBMs for the U.S. Navy in 1943; 410 in 1944; and 379 through the end of 1945.

The third American flying boat of World War II was the follow-on to the PBY. Consolidated's PB2Y Coronado was a four-engine giant weighing 20 tons empty, with a 4,000-mile range. Delivered to the fleet a year before Pearl Harbor, its production run amounted to 176 aircraft plus another 41 specifically built as PB2Y-3R transports. Coronado combat employment was almost wholly in the Pacific, where its exceptional range was most valued.

Part of the reason for the small Coronado acquisition was Consolidated's excellent PB4Y series. Originally simply "blue B-24s," the Liberators provided to the navy by the army air force immediately proved themselves on both sides of the Atlantic. Their speed, range, and versatility made them prime candidates for antisubmarine use.

However, specific naval requirements led to the single-tail PB4Y-2 Privateer variant, which appeared in 1943 and joined fleet squadrons in early 1944. Because patrol planes operated at relatively low altitudes, the PB4Y-2 did not require the B-24's turbo superchargers, permitting more fuel and armament to be added.

With 977 PB4Y-1s and 740 "dash twos," some 1,700 Consolidated bombers served U.S. Navy and Marine Corps squadrons, including photographic variants.

Lockheed broke into the patrol-plane market with the PV series of twin-engine attack aircraft. Developed from the RAF Hudson bomber, PV-1 Venturas were U.S. Army B-34s delivered in late 1942. The dash two Harpoon was a

A ground crewman signals to start number three engine of this Norfolk-based PB4Y-1, c. December 1943. Atlantic Fleet Liberator squadrons scored their first U-boat kill 5 November 1942, one month after initial delivery of the PB4Y. *USN photo*

One of the most important modifications of the navy Liberators was the PB4Y-1P long-range reconnaissance photo version. Redesignated P4Y-1P in 1951 when the bombing designation was abandoned by the navy, the -1P was the longest-serving model of the Liberator and was used until 1956 when VJ-62 retired the last one. A VD-2 PB4Y-1P in flight, c. 1945. *USN photo, courtesy Clay Jansson*

A maintenance crew performs a propeller change on a Norfolk-based PB4Y-1, c. 1943. *USN photo, courtesy Don Montgomery*

PB4Ys were a popular airframe for navy research and development facilities until long after World War II. This PB4Y-1 BuNo 32309 was used at the Naval Air Modification Unit at NAF Johnsville, Pennsylvania, for testing glide bombs. *Balogh, courtesy Dave Mendar*

new aircraft: bigger, longer ranged, and generally more capable. Its wholly naval use was emphasized by a new name as well, as the PV-2 reached navy squadrons in early 1944.

PV-1s represented the largest patrol-plane acquisition of the war when 985 were purchased from Vega Aircraft during 1943. Thereafter the annual "buy" was more than 400 Venturas and PV-2s, both in 1944 and 1945.

BATTLE OF THE ATLANTIC

Fast, rugged, and heavily armed, PVs were popular with their crews. They proved potent adversaries for enemy submarines and maritime aircraft, but it was far from

In 1943 Consolidated modified three B-24Ds into a new single-tail version for the navy, designated PB4Y-2 and renamed Privateer. The new aircraft had a longer fuselage, single vertical stabilizer, and different engine nacelles, while retaining the same wing and landing gear of the Liberator. *Convair photo*

VB-109 flew the first land-based missions against Okinawa from Saipan 14 July 1944 in their PB4Y-2s. They also launched Bat glide bombs on a raid at Balikpapan 23 April 1944 for the only combat use of this weapon. VB-109 PB4Y-2 "Poison Ivy" at Camp Kearney in June 1945. *Lou Darden, courtesy Jim Sullivan*

a one-sided conflict. No better example came out of the war than the sanguinary clashes the PatRons logged off the North American coast during 1943. In that period the U-boat master, Adm. Karl Doenitz, promulgated his "fight back" tactic with heavier 20- and 37-mm antiaircraft armament on his "seawolves." It proved temporarily effective: from June to November, at least eight U.S. Navy patrol planes were lost to U-boat gunfire, including three PBMs, three PB4Ys, and two PVs. American casualties amounted to more than 50 dead in these hard-fought engagements, as few aircrews survived the destruction of their patrol planes.

One example of the fight that a surfaced U-boat could put up occurred in the Caribbean on 6 August. Attacked by PBMs of VP-204 and -205, *U-615* shot down one, damaged three more, and inflicted mortal damage on a blimp of ZP-21. Battered by bombing and strafing, the submarine limped away to be sunk by a destroyer the next day.

Probably the hardest-fought battle was a six-hour shootout on 7 August 1943. Two PVs of VB-128 at Floyd Bennett Field, New York, attacked the surfaced *U-566* and were shot down, with a loss of at least seven air crew. Another Ventura from NAS Quonset Point, Rhode Island, was involved, while a VB-211 from Elizabeth City, New Jersey, was damaged in repeated runs when its depth charges failed to release. The submarine returned to its French base, though it was sunk by a British aircraft on the next patrol.

ACROSS THE PACIFIC

"P-boats" also provided sterling service in the vast reaches of the Pacific. From the first day of the war, Patrol Wing Ten in the Philippines was heavily involved as its two squadrons flew repeated sorties with diminishing support. VP-101 and -102 conducted searches, sank at least one ship and damaged three more between December 1941 and February 1942. The lopsided odds, however, finally forced a withdrawal to the Dutch East Indies and finally to Australia.

Catalinas proved their worth in subsequent battles, most notably at Midway in June 1942 and throughout the Guadalcanal campaign of 1942–1943. Knowing the odds of tracking an enemy carrier force with a combat air patrol, PBY crews typically signed off their contact reports with a Morse Code "NNK" (Nan-Nan-King in the phonetic alphabet) for "notify next of kin."

However, the lumbering "Cat" showed that it had claws. Bombing and torpedo attacks were successfully conducted by day and night, and the legendary Black Cat squadrons proved doubly effective. Dedicated to nocturnal attack missions and aided by radar, the Black Cats dogged Japanese shipping from the Solomons to the Philippines. Beginning in late 1942, VP-12 initiated Black Cat operations in the Solomons, blazing a nocturnal trail to be followed by other Catalina squadrons over the next three years. It was a trail lit by the fires of Japanese ships and bases set ablaze by marauding PBYs, but the Black Cats risked danger from other sources as well. Returning to its base in the Philippines in late 1944, a VP-33 aircraft was taken under fire by "friendly" forces with itchy trigger fingers. The PBY was so thoroughly holed that it sank on landing, providentially without loss of life.

Certainly no seaplane mission was more admired by other airmen than "Dumbo" rescue missions. The classic example was Lt. Nathan Gordon's rescue of three bomber crews from Kavieng Harbor in February 1944. Somehow getting his overloaded Catalina airborne amid artillery fire from shore, the VP-34 pilot saved 15 USAAF airmen from certain death or capture. His exceptional effort was recognized with a Medal of Honor while his crew also was decorated.

A posthumous "CMH" went to the CO of VPB-102, Lt. Comdr. Bruce Van Voorhis, killed with his entire PB4Y crew while attacking a remote Japanese base in the Carolines in July 1943.

Liberators and Privateers pursued Japanese shipping in the Western Pacific, flying long-range, low-level missions from the Philippines. Throughout the war, patrol planes were credited with some 300 enemy aircraft shot down, and several PB4Y crews rated as "aces." Even the huge, lumbering Coronado splashed Japanese aircraft as aggressive Lt. John Wheatley of VP-13 caught two Mitsubishi G4M Bettys in his PB2Y while operating from Guam. Additional VP missions included mining, reconnaissance, and electronic countermeasures.

LEATHERNECK PATROL BOMBERS

The Marine Corps also made good use of twin-engine patrol bombers in a variety of Pacific campaigns. First up was the Lockheed PV-1 modified for the night fighter role. The speedy Ventura lent itself to the complex mission, with good performance and heavy armament, plus the advantage of two engines and a three-man crew to share the workload. VMF(N)-531 used PV-1s modified with air-to-air radar sets to intercept Japanese nocturnal raiders in the upper Solomon Islands. Between November 1943 and May 1944, five of Col. Frank H. Schwable's Ventura crews were credited with 12 confirmed kills on hostile bombers and floatplanes.

The leathernecks' primary patrol bomber was another twin-engine, twin-tail design: North American's

Designed in 1937, the Martin PBM Mariner fought throughout World War II in a variety of roles. First deliveries of the big seaplane were to VP-55 on 1 September 1940. A total of 1,366 Mariners were accepted by the navy and the type served until July 1956 with VP-50 as its last squadron. A VP-56 PBM-1, in prewar markings, is photographed over Baltimore in 1941. *Rudy Arnold*

Martin's PBM fought in both the Atlantic and Pacific, but probably their greatest battles were against Nazi U-boats in the Atlantic and Caribbean. Increased anti-aircraft armament on the U-boats took a toll on ASW patrol bombers, and at least eight of them were shot down by U-boat gunfire, including three PBMs, three PB4Ys, and two PVs. These are Atlantic Fleet PBM-3 and -3Ss at NAS Norfolk, c. 1944–1945. *USN photo*

A PDM-3D of Fleet Air Wing One is serviced at Saipan during 1945. PBM-3Cs and subsequent models were characterized by a huge search radar doom just aft of the cockpit, *USN photo*

Below: During the Okinawa campaign, the largest seaplane force in history was assembled at Kerama Retto anchorage, in the Ryuku Islands. Nearly 90 PBMs from 9 squadrons were there, supported by 15 seaplane tenders. A PBM-5 is about to be hoisted on board a tender at Kerama Retto, c. April–July 1945. *USN photo*

A beaching crew washes corrosive saltwater off this PBM-3 at NAS Norfolk, after recovery from the bay, c. 1942–1943. *USN photo*

During World War II the navy made extensive use of flying boats and land-based bombers. The units were designated VP and VB (VPB after 1 October 1944) to cover their missions of long-range reconnaissance and heavy attack. Between 1936 and 1945, the navy bought 4,500 land-based patrol bombers, one of which was Lockheed's PV-1 Ventura. Additionally, 4,000 seaplanes were acquired. *Lockheed photo*

The Marines used Lockheed's PV-1 Ventura in a unique role in the Pacific as a night fighter. VMF(N)-531 operated PV-1s modified with radar and with six .50-caliber guns in the nose. Pictured here are VMF(N)-153 Venturas at Vella Vella, Solomon Islands, c. January 1944. *Herbert W. Price, courtesy E. S. Holmberg*

VMF(N)-531 "Gray Ghosts" PV-1 displays its four night-kill record at Vella Vella, c. January 1944. The squadron claimed at least 12 kills. *Herbert W. Price, courtesy E. S. Holmberg*

Below:
Lockheed produced an improved model of the PV as the PV-2 Harpoon. First squadron deliveries of this model began in March 1944. *Lockheed photo*

Ordnance crew loads bombs into a PV-1 in the Aleutians, c. summer 1943. *USN photo, courtesy Stan Piet*

The primary Marine Corps patrol bomber in World War II was the North American B-25 Mitchell, designated PBJ in naval service. Navy suffix designations corresponded with the AAF designations, i.e., B-25C=PBJ-1C, B-25D=PBJ-1D, etc. The marines' first combat with the Mitchell was with VMB-413 in March 1944 at Rabaul. VMB-413 PBJ-1Ds on a mission from Emirou Island, c. 1944. *USMC photo*

PBJ-1G and –H Mitchells had a 75-mm cannon mounted in the nose, in addition to as many as eight forward-firing .50-caliber machine guns, to increase their attack capabilities. Here, a PBJ-1H is on a North American test flight c. 1944. *North American photo*

B-25. Designated PBJ in naval service, the Mitchell was obtained directly from the Army Air Force in 1943 with total acquisitions running to 700 aircraft. The B-25C, D, G, H, and J models were identified as PBJ-1C, D, G, H, and J respectively, with nearly 500 aircraft among the latter two variants. The "strafing nose" models with as many as 14 .50-caliber machine guns and a 75-mm cannon were devastatingly effective on surface targets up to and including destroyers. Marine Mitchells of VMB-413 entered combat in March 1944, attacking air and naval facilities at Rabaul, New Britain. The PBJs specialized in night missions that kept the pressure on the Japanese defenders round the clock. Subsequently PBJs also operated in the Philippines and from Okinawa during 1945.

VMB-612 under Lt. Col. Jack Cram flew PBJs from Iwo Jima beginning in early April 1945, just as the Okinawa operation got under way. The Mitchells, now 750 miles from Japan, began long-range missions by day and night. Radar permitted them to find enemy ships at night, and the PBJ's potent armament, including rockets, began taking a toll. Additionally, the Mitchells carried big 11.75-inch Tiny Tim rockets, which contributed to the squadron's total of five ships sunk and more than 50 damaged.

Though patrol-plane production declined during the war, all five main types were still being delivered on VJ-Day: PBYs, PB2Ys, PB4Ys, PBMs, and PVs. The greatest single year's acquisition occurred in 1943 when the U.S. Navy obtained 2,193 patrol planes in addition to foreign purchases. Over the next two years, VP acquisition declined to about 1,500 per annum, with PVs and PB4Ys dominating.

In June 1945 the navy had 4,054 patrol bombers: 1,684 "P-boats" and 2,370 land-based bombers. Though usually overshadowed by their carrier-borne counterparts, the PatRons logged a truly world war. They flew in some of the worst weather on the planet, most notably in the Aleutian Islands and the expanse of the North Atlantic. Patrol-plane crews often logged 16-hour missions in which the greatest enemy was boredom, staring at thousands of square miles of sea and sky. But they performed vital service: locating enemy forces, attacking bases, harassing submarines, and perhaps most notably saving fellow aviators from the merciless grasp of the sea.

Appendices

U.S. Navy Dive and Torpedo Bombers, 1937–1945

Aircraft	Built	Remaining 2000
Curtiss SB2C/SBF/ SBW/A-25	7,139	5
Douglas SBD/A-24	5,936	25
Douglas TBD	130	0
Grumman TBF/TBM	9,837	91
Vought SB2U/V-156	260	1
Total	23,302	122

Bibliography

Bibliography

Francillon, René J. *Japanese Aircraft of the Pacific War*. UK: Putnam, 1979.

Franks, Norman, and Eric Zimmerman. *U-Boat Versus Aircraft*. London: Grub Street, 1998.

Gallery, Daniel V. *U-505*. New York: Paperback Library, 1968.

Grossnick, Roy, et al. *United States Naval Aviation 1910–1995*. Washington, D.C.: Naval Historical Center, 1997.

Heinemann, Edward H., and Rosario Rausa. *Ed Heinemann, Combat Aircraft Designer*. Annapolis, MD: Naval Institute Press, 1980.

Larkins, William T. *U.S. Navy Aircraft 1921–1941; U.S. Marine Corps Aircraft 1914–1959*. New York: Orion Books, 1988.

Lundstrom, John. *The First Team: Pacific Naval Air Combat from Pearl Harbor to Midway*. Annapolis, MD: Naval Institute Press, 1984.

Tillman, Barrett. *Avenger at War*. UK: Ian Allan, Ltd., 1979.

— *Carrier Battle in the Philippine Sea*. St. Paul, MN: Phalanx Pub. Co., 1994.

— *SB2C Units in World War II*. UK: Osprey Books, 1997.

— *SBD Units in World War II*. UK: Osprey Books, 1998.

— "Douglas TBD: the Maligned Warrior." *The Hook*, August 1990.

Wagner, Ray. *American Combat Aircraft (2nd edition)*. New York: Doubleday, 1982.

Index